She Shall Be Called Woman

VOLUME 2 • SECOND EDITION

Edited by Sheila Jones and Linda Brumley

She Shall Be Called Woman

VOLUME 2 • SECOND EDITION

Powerful Insights
from New Testament Women

DPI

DISCIPLESHIP
PUBLICATIONS
INTERNATIONAL

She Shall Be Called Woman
New Testament Women
Volume 2—Second Edition

©1995, 1998 by Discipleship Publications International
One Merrill Street, Woburn, MA 01801

All Scripture quotations, unless indicated, are taken from
the HOLY BIBLE, NEW INTERNATIONAL VERSION.
Copyright © 1973, 1978, 1984 by International Bible Society.
Used by permission of Zondervan Publishing House.
All rights reserved.

The "NIV" and "New International Version" trademarks
are registered trademarks in the United States Patent
Trademark Office by the International Bible Society.
Use of either trademarks requires the permission
of the International Bible Society.

Cover and layout design: Chris Costello
Cover image © 1998 PhotoDisc, Inc.

Printed in the United States of America

ISBN 1-57782-067-3

DEDICATION

To Elena McKean—
one who has the heart of Mary.

CONTENTS

INTRODUCTION 9

NEW TESTAMENT TIMES 12

BEFORE YOU START 17

1 ELIZABETH A Childlike Heart 18
   SHEILA JONES

2 MARY, MOTHER OF JESUS Chosen by God 25
   JOYCE ARTHUR

3 ANNA THE PROPHETESS Lifelong Devotion 31
   MARCIA LAMB

4 MARY MAGDALENE A Woman Repossessed 38
   GERI LAING

5 HERODIAS She Did It Her Way 44
   ADRIENNE SCANLON

6 SINFUL WOMAN An Outpouring of Faith 50
   TAMMY FLEMING

7 BLEEDING WOMAN The Touch of Faith 56
   ERICA KIM

8 THE WIDOW OF NAIN God's Specialty: The Impossible 60
   GLORIA BAIRD

9 MARY OF BETHANY Choose This Day 66
   KIM SAPP

10 MARTHA Open Home, Discipled Heart 71
   EMMA CAUSEY

11 SAMARITAN WOMAN Thirst for Righteousness 75
   DONNA LAMB

12 JOANNA A Gutsy Follower 80
   LINDA BRUMLEY

13 WIDOW AT THE TEMPLE Out of Her Poverty 85
   DIANE OTTENWELLER

14 MOTHER OF BLIND MAN I Will Not Fear 90
   JANET MARKS

15 SYROPHOENICIAN WOMAN Such Great Faith 95
   KAREN LOUIS

16 PILATE'S WIFE Act on Truth.. 99
   CATHY MARUTZKY

17 SAPPHIRA The Fruit of Deception... 104
   JOYCE (LEE) TAN

18 MARY, MOTHER OF JOHN MARK A Giving Heart 109
   GERI LAING

19 RHODA Opportunity Knocks 116
   LAVONIA DRABOT

20 SALOME, MOTHER OF JAMES AND JOHN True Greatness 120
   JUDY WEGER

21 DORCAS An Open-Heart Policy 126
   NADINE TEMPLER

22 LYDIA Bought for Eternity 132
   BARBARA PORTER

23 PRISCILLA Sold Out, Not Burned Out 137
   CARMEN GARCIA BENTLEY

24 DRUSILLA AND BERNICE Twisted Sisters 143
   EMMA SCOTT

25 WEAK-WILLED WOMEN Always Learning, Never Knowing........ 148
   KAY MCKEAN

26 EUODIA AND SYNTYCHE Work It Out! 152
   JACKIE MCGRATH

27 EUNICE AND LOIS Faithful Forerunners 156
   GLORIA BAIRD

28 PHILIP'S DAUGHTERS Chosen by God 162
   EMILY BRINGARDNER

29 PHOEBE Simply a Servant 168
   MARIA ROGERS

BIBLIOGRAPHY 172

APPLICATION.. 173
   Your Personal Response

INTRODUCTION

Jesus had a heart for people. He wanted everyone to follow him and have a relationship with him—men and women. Both played an intimate and integral role in his ministry. The practice of a rabbi having followers was common, but having women followers was anything but common. In fact, it was radically uncommon.

Jesus compassionately touched women who were considered untouchable by other religious leaders of the day. He was touched by women who would have been rebuked for their audacity by pious rabbis but were emotionally and physically healed by the one who came to seek and save the lost.

A woman bore him out of union with the Spirit of God. He who created all things was born of his very creation. He designed the womb that protected him and the breasts that nursed him. In so doing, he was an example of complete humility and trust—God in the form of a helpless child. The Father entrusted his own Son to the nurturing love of one of his created beings—Mary, God's chosen woman.

Women sat at his feet to learn the secrets of God, an honor culturally afforded only to male disciples. But Jesus did not respond to the dictates of culture. He responded to the will of his Father, and he extended an understanding of that will to all who "had ears to hear." And many women who were eager for a relationship with their God had ears to hear.

The women in the New Testament were honored by God from beginning to end. Elizabeth, through the Spirit, first proclaimed the conception of God in flesh as Mary approached, newly pregnant:

> "Blessed are you among women, and blessed is the child you will bear! But why am I so favored, that the mother of my Lord should come to me?" (Luke 1:42-43).

Mary of Magdala, close friend, supporter and devoted follower of Jesus, first proclaimed his resurrection:

> "Go instead to my brothers and tell them, 'I am returning to my Father and your Father, to my God and your God.'" Mary Magdalene went to the disciples with the news: "I have seen the Lord!" And she told them that he had said these things to her (John 20:17-18).

After the ascension of Jesus and the birth of his church, women like the sisters, Drusilla and Bernice, who were pampered and self-centered, were honored by God to hear the message of Jesus through the earnest pleadings of Paul (Acts 24:24-25; 25:23-32). They, among others, did *not* have ears to hear.

But, thankfully, there were women like Lydia, Priscilla and Phoebe, who left all to proclaim the risen Lord, giving of their means and risking their lives. Their faith and leadership in the early church afforded help to many and gave credibility to a new movement finding its way through the litter of cultural and spiritual injustice and prejudice.

God's plan was for men and women to work side by side in spreading the good news of his grace, and Jesus lived out that plan (Luke 8:1-3). Following the teaching and example of his Lord, Paul also labored along with his sisters, calling Euodia and Syntyche "fellow workers" and saying that they "contended at my side in the cause of the gospel" (Romans 16; Philippians 4:2-3). Although the leadership roles of apostle, evangelist and elder were reserved for men, women led other women and had a great influence on the male leaders as they worked alongside them. Paul was clear in delineating the roles given only to males in the structure of the early church, but he was also clear in stating the equality of believers in the kingdom of God:

> You are all sons of God through faith in Christ Jesus, for all of you who were baptized into Christ have been clothed with Christ. There is neither Jew nor Greek, slave nor free, male nor female, for you are all one in Christ Jesus. If you belong to Christ, then you are Abraham's seed, and heirs according to the promise (Galatians 3:26-29).

Paul was not in any way patronizing women; rather he was reflecting the respect pouring out to them from their creator, God himself.

Just as we learned from our sisters of the Old Testament in Volume I, so we learn from our first-century sisters in this volume. These are women who spent time with Jesus in the flesh and with the apostles who spoke his inaugural message. These are women who felt firsthand the earth-shattering effect of the cross of Jesus, the pivotal event of history. As in the previous volume, we view the composite—

the bad, the worst, the good, the best—of our womanhood. We learn the mistakes to avoid, the sins to renounce, the truth to obey, and the grace to proclaim. We grow along with the writers as they share their responses to the characters they have come to "know" over the course of a month's prayer, meditation and study time.

We gain perspective on who God meant us to be as women—not possessing a certain body build or personality or sense of humor or thought process, but possessing a heart humbled before our God. We see how to realize our potential to affect the lives of others and make an indelible mark in the record of history for eternity.

Let's learn from our sisters who lived 2,000 years ago but were just like the woman next door, the girl down the hall, the coworker in the adjoining cubicle. Let's learn so we can grow personally to trust and to please God. And let's learn so we can help others to do the same. Let's be changed so we, along with our brothers, can change the world.

-Sheila Jones

NEW TESTAMENT TIMES

God was silent for some 400 years. During the time between the ending of the Old Testament and the beginning of the New, not one prophet spoke his message to the people. But secular historians left records of significant changes in the social, political and religious climate of the world at that time. God had caused the Persian king, Cyrus, (who reigned from 559 to 529 B.C.) to release the captive Jews and send them back to Jerusalem to rebuild their city, its wall and its holy temple. It is there that the Old Testament story ends. The final chapters recording the history of the Jews give the Bible student no clue as to the formation of the institutions and customs that are introduced without explanation in the New Testament story: rabbis, synagogues, the Sanhedrin, Scribes, Pharisees, Sadducees, kings called Herod and a non-Jewish governor of a Jewish state. How did it all come about?

At Just the Right Time

The God of the nations used 400 years of dramatic events to accomplish his purposes. He wanted to prepare the way for his Son to become flesh and to introduce the new way to God. The key players are familiar to us, but not from the pages of the Bible: Alexander the Great, Ptolemy, Cleopatra, Marc Antony, Julius Caesar. They all played roles in the drama that set the stage for the world to receive its Savior. God's task in the Old Testament was narrow— one nation in the spotlight, one language for his written law, one central location. But as God prepared for his new law to reach every nation, timing was everything:

> And he made known to us the mystery of his will according to his good pleasure, which he purposed in Christ, to be put into effect when the times will have reached their fulfillment—to bring all things in heaven and on earth together under one head, even Christ (Ephesians 1:9-10).

Persia was the dominant world power from 536 until 323 B.C., when Alexander the Great, believing himself to be a god, expanded the borders of the kingdom of Greece through Palestine, Persia, Egypt and India. Greek culture permeated those subjugated nations, and the Greek language became the common language of the world. The Greeks made pace-setting, world-impacting advances in art, architecture, astronomy, math, medicine, literature and philosophy. Greek scholarship was so highly regarded that even after Rome conquered Greek territories, all formal tutoring was done in classical Greek.

In Just the Right Language

Typically, any given language evolves with its culture. Over time, some words take on entirely new meanings as common usage dictates definition. But God had a plan for Greek, the language in which he would communicate his new law. First, he caused it to develop a precise and expansive delineation of verb tenses and noun genders. Then, he caused the language used in formal education, classical Greek, to stand still, frozen in form, distinct from the common Greek spoken by the people. How perfect an arrangement for a God who wanted to precisely communicate his will for man for all languages, for all generations. Scholars could forever refer to that unchanged, classical language to check the exact meaning of the very words of God.

Even the old Hebrew Scriptures were translated into Greek. The Egyptian city of Alexandria, which Alexander the Great had named after himself, was a great center of Greek learning. It held the world's largest library during the reign of the Ptolemies. It is said to have contained over 700,000 scrolls. In the third century B.C., 70 Jewish scholars were brought in from Jerusalem to translate the Old Testament into Greek. This translation was called the *Septuagint*. By the time Jesus began his ministry and was quoting from the old law, even the Gentiles could understand.

All Roads Led to Rome

After the death of Alexander the Great, his kingdom was, for a time, divided between his four generals. One of these was Ptolemy, who ruled over the area of Palestine and Egypt and was succeeded by his offspring (Cleopatra was a Ptolemy) until the Roman invasion in 63 B.C.

If the Greeks were the brains, the Romans were the brawn. The powerful Roman army pushed into Europe, the Middle East and northern Africa. When the Roman soldiers were not fighting, they were building roads linking all parts of their empire. These roads were so well engineered that portions remain in use 2,000 years later. A common language, accessible roadways and waterways—the influence of *a* kingdom and *the* kingdom could spread more easily and rapidly than ever!

Captivity Brought Changes

The years of captivity had been hard on the Jews, who longed for independence and national sovereignty. Those dispersed among foreign nations built synagogues in their communities and relied on copies of the original writings of the Old Testament made by scribes. They substituted the study of the law for sacrifice and the other rituals of worship which could only take place at the temple in Jerusalem. Rabbis (or teachers) led the worship and study and added their own writings and traditions to the law. Even the Jews who returned to Jerusalem and rebuilt the temple continued to incorporate the customs of captivity into their culture.

Sects developed among them as different ideologies arose, many from other cultural influences. The most prominent sects were the Pharisees and the Sadducees. The Pharisees were legalistic and self-righteous. The Sadducees were unspiritual, but wealthy and influential. The Jewish equivalent of the Supreme Court was called "the Sanhedrin." This decision-making body of 70 members was made up of Sadducees, Pharisees, priests, scribes and elders. They could pontificate but were often unable to enforce their decisions because they didn't control the law in their own land—Rome did.

The Need for a Savior

The Jews longed for a savior from Roman control. They were eager to find a patriot like Judas the Maccabee, who had thrown off Syrian domination a century and a half earlier (though only for a few years). When Jesus came on the scene, they saw in him the power to rally the people and restore the national rule to Israel. God *did* send them a savior, and he *was* Jesus, but he was a Savior from sin and death, not the Romans. Some resented the implication that they needed a Savior from sin. They were not interested in a spiritual kingdom. As the truth of his message unfolded, they resented the prospect that they were spiritual equals with Gentiles...and slaves...and WOMEN!! This new order of things was very threatening—the heritage and promises that had once been exclusively theirs were now extended to all!

After years of meticulous planning and painstaking labor, God gave birth to his church. The first century ushered in the era of "the last days" spoken of by the prophets:

> In the last days
> the mountain of the LORD's temple will be established
>   as chief among the mountains;
> it will be raised above the hills,
>   and all nations will stream to it.
> Many peoples will come and say,
> "Come, let us go up to the mountain of the LORD,
>   to the house of the God of Jacob.
> He will teach us his ways,
>   so that we may walk in his paths."
> The law will go out from Zion,
>   the word of the LORD from Jerusalem (Isaiah 2:2-3).

-Linda Brumley

BEFORE YOU START
Know Where You Are Going

◆ Each chapter is divided into five sections:

1. Scripture reference
2. Historical background (written by the editors)
3. Character study
4. Writer's personal response
5. Focus question

◆ The chapters were written assuming that you will have read the scripture references *first*. As tempting as it is to skip over them and jump into the meat of the chapter, don't give in! *Read the scriptures first.* We promise you the text will have infinitely more meaning if you do. Also, reading the references enables you to discern the parts of the chapters that are fictionalized to help bring the characters to life.

◆ To help you apply what you are reading, we have included an "Application" section in the back of the book with specific questions to ask after each chapter. Be prepared to see yourself in the mirror of the Word!

1. As you make personal application, you can write a brief response in the space given. Boil it down to a one- or two-sentence insight or commitment. The more simple your response, the better your grasp of what God wanted you to understand.

2. These application questions can also be used in small group discussion situations. It is encouraging and unifying to read and discuss the chapters along with others. We learn more about our character when we are open to others' input. Also, we grow more in our character when we are open to others' support.

1

ELIZABETH
A Childlike Heart

Luke 1:1-80

Being a priest of God was an honor. You could not buy it or earn it. You were simply born to it—you had to be a descendent of Aaron. Certain restrictions were placed on priests, especially when it came to marriage.

A priest had to marry a virgin who was not the daughter of a former slave. She also had to be a true Jew, not a proselyte. If a priest were widowed without children, he could not marry a woman who was "incapable." In addition to these restrictions, the high priest had to marry a woman who also belonged to a priestly family.*

What a difficult situation it must have been for the barren wife of a priest. But the God who parted the Red Sea delights in changing difficult situations.

◆

She glanced at the familiar shadow of the tree behind their house. Calculating the position of the sun, she knew it was around 4:00 in the afternoon. Her husband should be home soon since the walk from Jerusalem took the better part of a day. She wiped her hands on a nearby cloth, glancing absently at the age spots that had begun to show in the last year. She shook the flour from her garment and placed the freshly baked bread on the table. She wanted the meal to be ready when he returned, knowing he would be tired and hungry.

Walking out the door, she shaded her eyes against the slanted rays of the sun and strained to see down the road. A few carts passed and several small groups of laborers. Finally she saw him—a familiar figure in the distance. His determined, head-down, no-nonsense gait always notified her of his approach. Although he was beginning to show signs of aging, he was still a strong man with a confident stride.

As he came closer, she began to feel a certain uneasiness. What was the matter? When he was close enough for her to clearly see his features, she

*Emil Schurer, *A History of the Jewish People in the Times of Jesus Christ* (Peabody, Massachusetts: Hendrickson) 207.

saw a look on his face she had never seen before—not in all their years of married life. Elizabeth, an older woman herself, had known her share of tragedy. She braced herself for whatever news he was bringing. But she could never have prepared herself for the incredible happening he would soon share with her. As he stood before her, silent and moving his hands wildly, she would soon understand that what she had misread as tragedy was really the most wonderful news she would ever receive.

The Visitation

What frustration Zechariah must have felt as he tried to communicate to his bewildered wife what had happened to him a few days earlier at the temple. As a priest, a descendant of Aaron, he served with his division one week out of every six. He had been assigned by lot the duty of offering the incense—first thing each morning and last thing each night. While on duty, an angel appeared to him—not an everyday occurrence, even for a priest! Uneasy and fearful, Zechariah stared dumbfounded. The angel comforted him and brought him a message of hope, of answered prayer, of a son who would lead the people back to God.

Unfortunately, Zechariah allowed his amazement to give birth to a sinful attitude. Standing before the messenger of the God of Abraham, Isaac and Jacob, he displayed a "show-me" attitude. In the annals of Hebrew history, others had questioned God and were simply answered. How did he *sin* in his questioning? In *unbelief.* The angel said, "And now you will be silent and not able to speak until the day this happens, because you did not believe my words..." (Luke 1:20). Unbelief spawns arrogance, cynicism and ingratitude. In the presence of *the* sign, his intellect cried out for *a* sign. As a result, he was disciplined by the Most High God as he stood in his temple before his altar and his messenger. God's reproof came swiftly. No *ifs.* No *ands.* No *buts.* Punctuated by the statement, "I am Gabriel. I stand in the presence of God..." (Luke 1:19).

Zechariah must have reentered the courtyard a changed man. Totally humbled, totally repentant, and totally convinced. A righteous man was being purified to receive and raise a messenger for God.

The Wait

Zechariah and Elizabeth are described as "upright in the sight of God" (Luke 1:6). They were devout and sincere—both descendants of Aaron. He, a priest; she, the daughter of a priest. The fact that she also was from a priestly family would have added to their already respected position in the community.

What must Elizabeth have felt as her husband laboriously communicated to her without words the incredible news he had received? Her mind must have flashed back to memories of her father telling her about Abraham and Sarah, about the astounding news they too received from a messenger of God. Sarah laughed to think of having a child—and yet, Elizabeth's faith had the benefit of knowing what had happened to Sarah. She *did* have a child in her old age, and that child became the father of Israel, Elizabeth's nation. How foolish it would be for her not to believe. God had once again chosen to work his will in the body of one who was "well along in years." Miracle of miracles! *She* was to have a baby!

What wonder, as she experienced the first stirrings of life within! The breasts that had sagged with age were now full and round, preparing to nurse the child she had thought she would never have. For decades she had rejoiced with and comforted pregnant friends. She had listened to their good-natured complaints of kicks in the ribs, of bladders urgent with the pressure of an enlarging uterus, of the elasticity of skin stretched as never before. Now, it was happening to her!

Even in the excitement and wonder of it all, she could not help but feel some fear, some sense of the strangeness of it all. This body she had known and cared for over the years had never done things it was doing now. She probably felt somewhat out of control, but then she would surely remember that the gift was from God, and he would bring that gift to term and deliver it. In all the wonder, strangeness and lack of control, she was filled with inexplicable joy. After years of prayer and hope, she had totally given up. Her ovaries had shriveled, her tubes had long since ceased to carry eggs to be fertilized. New life from the author of life. Something from nothing—the paradox of his nature.

The Visit

While Elizabeth was in her sixth month of pregnancy, the angel, Gabriel, made another visit—this time to her young relative, Mary of Nazareth. The news brought to Mary was even more incredible. She was a virgin and was to become pregnant without sexual union with a man. She was to bear God's Son—the Savior of his people.

Hearing that Elizabeth was also experiencing a miraculous pregnancy, Mary hurried to the hill country to visit her relative. What a joy for Elizabeth! With so many new things happening in her body, her heart, her soul, she longed to talk with her husband as she once had—when he was able to speak. The most incredible event was happening, and they could not speak of it together. With Mary there, she finally had someone with whom she could share her heart. Someone who would truly understand. Someone who was also bearing a miracle of God.

Zechariah must have struggled as he looked at his wife's expanding figure with awe and wonder—to sleep next to an unfolding miracle and not be able to praise God aloud was a discipline that would have grown more difficult each day. Yet, because of his devout heart before God, we can imagine that Zechariah did not harbor resentment toward a righteous God who disciplined only for his own good. God must have been preparing his faith so he could father a child who would grow to be a unique and powerful man of God.

As Mary first approached Elizabeth, the child in Elizabeth's womb kicked with exhilaration and anticipation in the presence of *Emmanuel*—"God with us"—in embryonic form. He had come to her, and she was honored beyond belief as the Spirit filled her:

> "Blessed are you among women and blessed is the child you will bear! But why am I so favored, that the mother of my Lord should come to me? As soon as the sound of your greeting reached my ears, the baby in my womb leaped for joy. Blessed is she who has believed that what the Lord has said to her will be accomplished" (Luke 1:42-45).

She spoke words from God himself; she was the first to announce the coming of the Messiah. The fruit of the Spirit within her was humility; she gladly accepted that the son of the older would serve and prepare the way for the son of the younger. There was no sign of pride, of competitiveness. If God wanted to work through a younger woman, then let it be. A humble mother would give birth to a humble son. In years to come, he also would be honored that Emmanuel came to him in the form of his younger cousin: "But one more powerful than I will come, the thongs of whose sandals I am not worthy to untie" (Luke 3:16).

It should be no surprise that Mary stayed for three months. Not only was she probably experiencing morning sickness, but she and Elizabeth had much to share. They must have daily shook their heads in amazement and compared notes on their progressing pregnancies.

How they must have held on to each other when she *did* leave. They must have looked deeply into each other's eyes, satisfied with the sense of shared wonder and faith—two ordinary women in an ordinary house experiencing something supernaturally extraordinary. They were each bearing sons who would affect the world for eternity.

The Birth

First labor, even when your child has been miraculously con-ceived, is *still* first labor. Elizabeth experienced the process of birth from a different perspective that day. She had undoubtedly attended others during their times of delivery. Now she was the one being attended. One last triumphant push, adrenaline pumping, forehead sweating...out he came—hairy and yelling at the top of his lungs. John, to be called the Baptist, emerged from the watery sac of protection and announced to the world, *I am here.* The Spirit within announced to the heavenly realms, *God is here, and he is ready to unfold the plan of the ages.* The forerunner of the Messiah was cleaned, wrapped in clean cloths, and placed in the trembling arms of his mother. A son. So long she had waited. Too soon she had given up. What did God have in store for this miracle baby? *I must have the heart of Hannah. I must give him back to God, my Samuel, his chosen.*

On the eighth day when the neighbors came for the circumcision, they assumed that he would take his father's name. After all, he was the firstborn, and surely to be the *lastborn!* But his mother, with conviction, said, "No! He is to be called John" (Luke 1:60).

She must be out of her mind. Her pregnancy has made her mad. To their amazement, Zechariah wrote on the slate, "His name is John" (Luke 1:63). Immediately, his captive tongue was loosed. Through the Spirit, he poured out praise to God...praise stored up for 10 long months in the heart of this new father of a prophet. The people marveled. The talk spread around the region. "What then is this child going to be?" (Luke 1:66).

Surely, Elizabeth, like Mary, pondered in her heart the words spoken by the angel concerning her son. She would see him "turn the hearts of the fathers to their children and the disobedient to the wisdom of the righteous—to make ready a people prepared for the Lord" (Luke 1:17). The humble and powerful son of this humble and grateful mother would eventually be beheaded for boldly speaking the truth of God to a king, and was surely welcomed home by *the* King. God gave her a gift and she gave him back, and they were both blessed in the giving.

Can Good Be Bad?

A heart filled with the Holy Spirit is grateful. Vulnerable. Child-like. This is Elizabeth as she greeted Mary. She was filled with gratitude and awe that the mother of her Lord would come to her. I need to be like this woman.

Her grateful heart moved her to be unguarded. She did not allow protective defenses to go up. Like a two-year-old, this mature woman poured out her heart...loudly. This challenges me. When I personally share my thoughts and feelings, I want my responses to be pre-washed, neatly packaged and delivered. Very safe. Very protected. No risks.

I tend to be *good* by not saying what I am really thinking and feeling in situations. My good is really *bad*. My good is really dishonesty. It becomes a barrier to my relationship with everyone in my life, including God. And Jesus came to show us, and everyone else, who we really are—in order to change us into his image. It is silly to act like I already *am* what I am supposed to be. I want to be like Jesus, but that only happens when I stop *sanitizing* myself *by* myself. I must consistently be open about who I am. God already knows anyway. And others cannot help me change or give me the encouragement I need if I am not real with them.

Emotions still scare me. I guess sometimes I'm afraid I won't be able to control them. And I much prefer to feel in control. I don't like to deal with things in front of people. I am afraid of what might come out, of what might have been caged up. I prefer to take my "bone" to the corner, away from others, and "chew" on it. When I get to the level of my emotional discomfort, I feel like a little kid. I do not feel like a mature mother, wife, writer and editor. Precisely the need! "Unless you change and become like little children, you will never enter the kingdom of heaven" (Matthew 18:3). The fear of the unknown is strong. But he who is in me is stronger. Jesus did come to set us free. And it is only when we are free that we can truly bear the burdens of others on whatever level they need us.

I do not want honesty at the expense of sensitivity. I also do not want deceit under the guise of discernment. But I would rather make a mistake than build an image. I am never more alive than when I am vulnerable. It is only then that I realize how much I need discipling by others and by God.

Elizabeth did not hold back in sharing her heart with Mary. Her childlike spirit is a call to all of us to lay down our defenses and to open up our hearts. Don't let fear, competitiveness or insecurity keep you from being all God wants you to be. God *is* faithful. He will fulfill his promise to you and me—just as he fulfilled his promise to Elizabeth.

Sheila Jones
Boston, USA

 Are you open or guarded in your relationships? Would you rather make a mistake and grow, or be unreal and build an image?

application questions on page 173

2

MARY
MOTHER OF JESUS
Chosen by God

Matthew 1:18-2:23; 12:46-50; 13:53-58; Mark 3:31-34;
Luke 1:26-56; 2:1-52; 8:19-21; 11:27-28;
John 2:1-11; 6:41-42; 19:25-27; Acts 1:12-14

The Jews were politically impotent in a land that belonged to them by divine right. Although Rome was a democratic state, the citizens of the conquered nations did not share in that democracy. Roman armies had marched into Jerusalem in 63 B.C. The Jews resented Rome's control and espoused a chip-on-the-shoulder faith, saying, "Our God will get you for this!"

Rome tolerated the Jews' religious idiosyncrasies as long as they paid their taxes and threatened no rebellion. To oversee these two stipulations, a governor (Pilate) and a king (Herod) were the arm of Rome in Israel. Their power was absolute. There were no cumbersome legalities like "due process" to restrict their authority where their foreign subjects were concerned. At their whim, they could arrest, torture, crucify. They could even issue edicts ordering infants to be murdered by soldiers. Roman officials could do whatever they wanted as long as Rome went unbothered.

Into this tense climate a Hebrew girl was born. Her family was poor and obscure, but she became the mother of a king. Her name was Mary.

◆

The time had come. Men and women, prophets and priests, Jews and Gentiles had been waiting. History and prophecy had been building to a climax. It was time for a change! The old must go; the new must come. But how? How would the Messiah, the Savior of mankind, enter into this unworthy world?

People's imaginations must have been going wild as they antici-pated this glorious event. Who would be the honored woman to bear the Son of God? Of course, she would be beautiful, rich and well-connected. Wait, what is this? There must be some mistake. Mary of Nazareth? Insignificant, unassuming, poor and unmarried Mary of Nazareth? What was God trying to accomplish through this outrageous venture? What did Mary possess that separated her from all the rest? In short—a willing spirit. She was willing to surrender her will to the will of God despite the cost. And the cost would be great! God, speaking through Simeon, warned Mary just after Jesus' birth:

> "This child is destined to cause the falling and rising of many in Israel, and to be a sign that will be spoken against, so that the thoughts of many hearts will be revealed. And a sword will pierce your own soul too" (Luke 2:34-35).

Not exactly the words a mother wants or expects to hear as she gazes proudly at her firstborn. These words she stored in her heart for safe keeping until their meaning became clear.

Willing to Give Birth

In the era of "planned parenthood" we are sensitive to the sacrifice made by Mary as she heard the angel's decree, "You will be with child and give birth to a son, and you are to give him the name Jesus" (Luke 1:31). The responses of today's woman might be: "You don't understand my situation!" "I'm not ready for this yet!" "What are my options?" "No way!" "*Jesus?* I'm not sure I like that name." "I have my rights! No one asked me about this." But Mary had the right response: "How *will* this be?" (Luke 1:34). Knowing it *would* happen, Mary, as a willing servant, surrendered instantly to God's plan.

Of course, it would cause much turmoil and embarrassment to her life. She was a virgin, an unmarried woman in a time when unfaithful women had few rights. She would surely be a disgrace to her family and her beloved fiancé Joseph. What about her reputation? What would happen to her marriage plans? The wedding and festivities that she had been dreaming of had now been tainted by this untimely intrusion.

Though these could have been her responses, Mary was obviously on a different wavelength. That is precisely why God chose her. She was not consumed with *her* life, *her* plans, *her* timing. Mary was a humble servant, aware of her lowly position and, undoubtedly, aware of God's omnipotence. Sure, becoming pregnant before she was married was not on her agenda, but who was she to interfere with the plans of God? "I am the Lord's servant...May it be to me as you have said" (Luke 1:38). She was not only willing in her actions, but was also willing in her heart—the hardest part. "My soul glorifies the Lord, and my spirit rejoices in God my Savior" (Luke 1:46-47). Mary knew that fearing the Lord meant *not giving in to fears*.

Even as the events of the birth unfolded, and Mary was denied the right to settle her "nesting instinct," she continued in her willingness. She gave birth in a barn far away from her friends and relatives, far away from the support that women long for when giving birth to their first child. Her infant was wrapped lovingly and placed unapologetically in an animal's feeding trough. She did not protest or emotionally cry out, *I have had enough, I can't take anymore!* Instead, she surrendered to her God, entrusting all to him and pondering it all in her heart.

Willing to Give Her Best

So, did she mindlessly go along for the ride? Did she stand back as God raised his Son in her household? What would be so hard about that? Hardly! She was given an immense amount of responsibility. She was expected to nurture, train, discipline and guide the Son of God from infancy to adulthood. Living under the same roof as Jesus was quite a challenge. All she could do was her best. Of course, her best in the face of perfection would fall miserably short. But, with her eyes on God and not on herself, Mary performed her duties with grace. Mary's pure heart surely must have been one of the reasons God had chosen her in the first place.

The role Jesus' earthly mother would play in his life is a rather complicated concept. Since the Scriptures tell us that John the Baptist was "filled with the Holy Spirit even from birth" (Luke 1:15), we can assume that "the fullness of the deity" (Colossians 2:9) lived in the bodily form of the newborn baby Jesus. God chose for Jesus to have a childhood—another bridge between humanity and divinity—to help us relate to Jesus. But how can a mother have influence over a child who is already perfect? Since it was crucial for God to choose a pure-hearted woman to rear his son, we can know that she would have the power to influence him. We can also know that she must have been challenged daily by her son's life.

As a preteen in the temple, Jesus amazed his mother with his spiritual understanding. What conflicting emotions she must have felt as she frantically searched for the son entrusted to her care, only to be reminded that he was God's Son too, and God had infinitely more power to watch over him and keep him safe.

Mary gave her best to Jesus and helped him to grow "in wisdom and stature, and in favor with God and men" (Luke 2:52). Even though he was full of the Spirit, he was not full grown in all these areas. She helped him navigate the waters of childhood and teen years.

Willing to Give Him Back

As he began his ministry, she, like the disciples, did not yet understand the scope of his mission. When she heard that he was so consumed with ministering to others that he was not even taking time to eat right, like a typical mother, she stepped up to "take charge" of the situation (Mark 3:20-21, 31-35). *Mother* often does know what is best, but not when her son is God in the flesh!

Jesus' correction was clear, loving and totally unsentimental, "Who are my mother and my brothers?. . .Whoever does God's will is *my* brother and sister and mother" (Mark 3:33, 35).

Through his words Mary was called to do God's will, to think as God thought about his Son's life, ministry and, eventually, death. She must have submitted humbly to that call, her support of his ministry being evident throughout the torture of the cross and the joy of the resurrection. Perhaps the most touching scene in the life of Mary is the picture of her standing at the foot of her son's cross. Of all the disciples present that day, Jesus' mother must have experienced the greatest pain. God had expected much of Mary, and Mary had given much. She had been willing to give birth to Jesus on one day and every day after that to give him her best. Now, in her aging years, God had called on her to give him back! This must have been the hardest test of all.

The memories of Jesus taking his first steps and calling out to her in the night must have come flooding into her mind. The powerful instinct of a mother to protect her child from all harm must have been almost too much to bear. And yet, Mary was willing. She knew from the beginning that Jesus foremost was *God's* Son. She understood her role and had been willing to submit to God, even to the bitter end. Jesus had been a blessing for her to enjoy and not a possession for her to hold.

Mary's complete submission of heart and soul were obvious by her presence at the cross. She might have been tempted not to witness it and avoid the terrible pain. But her spiritual focus and her trust in God's plan carried her through. Just as Mary had been willing to receive Jesus from God in the beginning, she was also unconditionally willing to give him back.

The "Willingness" Factor

I am continually learning new things as I grow through different stages of life. Praying and studying about Mary this month has revealed much to me about my personality and heart.

Mary was willing to give birth. For Christian women this is not usually a struggle! Timing may not always be ideal, but overall we view children as one of God's greatest blessings. I had a beautiful three-month-old baby boy when I found out I was once again pregnant. But I was still overjoyed, and Jessica has truly been a blessing to my life.

Mary, however, was a virgin! This was an impossible thing that had just been made possible by God—surprise! I had to ask myself, *How do I cope with surprises in my life? When I am asked to move to a different town to advance the kingdom, or to take on more responsibility when I already feel overwhelmed, how do I respond? How is my "willingness" factor then? Is "I am the Lord's servant" the first thought that pops into my mind?*

I remember in 1986, a few weeks before Christmas, I was confronted with one of these surprises in my life. Our plans to send a missionary family to Australia fell through at the very last minute. So it was decided that Douglas and I would move to Australia in two weeks' time! We spent Christmas packing and organizing. Our children were one-and-a-half and two-and-a-half years old. This was not what I had planned, but the Lord was calling on us, and we were willing to serve. The Lord really blessed that time in our lives, and I look back on it with the fondest of memories. We have had many similar events in our lives since then. My spirit has been tested again and again.

As my responsibilities have grown both in the church and at home, I have found it increasingly difficult to consistently give my best. I have definitely struggled with just keeping up at times.

Sometimes, *I can't take it anymore* has been my first reaction rather than, *May it be to me as you have said.* Of course, through prayer and basically "getting a grip," God has taught me that with him, all things are possible.

Mary's heart at the cross was the most convicting part of my study. I envisioned myself there and truly cannot comprehend how she survived it. She surrendered herself totally at this time, realizing that Jesus was truly the Son of God. What I realized is that each and every one of our children belongs to God more than they belong to us as mothers. It goes against my inner fiber as a mother to allow my children to suffer in any way. Moving back to the U.S.A., after having lived overseas for more than 10 years, has made me aware of how tempting and easy it is to make life comfortable for my children. I want them to excel in school and in sports, to have their own successful social lives and to have fun and play and be children. All these things are important, of course, but they can become major distractions from doing the simple will of God in my life (especially seeking and saving the lost) if I'm not very careful.

The most important questions for me as a Christian woman are: *How am I doing in my relationship with God? Am I powerfully fulfilling my purpose?* My concern is the same for my children. They often have to experience sacrifice and pain to accomplish these things.

Just yesterday I overheard my daughter sharing her faith with a girl in our neighborhood. The little girl was very uninterested, and it hurt Jessica's feelings. This is so important for her to experience, but it is not easy for me, as her mother, to witness it. Mary chose to witness the pain and suffering of her son on the cross, knowing it was God's will and was necessary for mankind. I am grateful for the incredible example she has set, and I want to imitate her in my mothering.

Praise God he chose Mary, a woman, to play such an important role in his plan for all time. I am grateful to Mary that she was willing to say *Yes* and give her best to God.

Joyce Arthur
Washington, DC, USA

FOCUS   What is your first response to the surprises in your life? Is it total surrender to God's plan for you?

application questions on page 173

3

ANNA THE PROPHETESS
Lifelong Devotion

Luke 2:36-38

When we think of prophets, most of us probably visualize powerful men with penetrating eyes and unruly beards. A prophet brought God's message to the people, both by foretelling and forthtelling truth. That is, they brought the truth of God to bear on present circumstances and on future happenings. We can sometimes forget, though, that the prophetic office was also held by women. In the tradition of Miriam, Huldah and Deborah, an old woman named Anna spoke the prophetic words of God during the first century B.C. and A.D. A widow who had committed her life to God, she was the first woman who proclaimed the presence and power of the Son of God in the flesh.

◆

In Luke 2:36-38, God preserves a moment in the life of Anna, the aged but vibrant prophetess. Because she was born during the "silent years" between the Old and New Testaments, little is known about her. However, the history of Israel during her lifetime and the triumphant outcome of the end of her life shed some light on her identity.

Perseverance

Anna was probably born around 100 B.C., 30 years after Jerusalem became its own political power under the (Maccabbean) Hasmoneon Empire. She grew up and was married during the reign of the cruel Jewish king, Aristobulus (103-76 B.C.). As was the custom, Anna probably married as a teenager, from 14 to 16 years old. Losing her life partner in her early twenties was an unexpected sorrow. Anna did not know that she would be widowed for 84 long years.

The personal pain of this young widow was compounded by an ungodly, religious authority figure. Unrighteous spiritual leaders give messages of discouragement, disillusionment and doubt. Anna chose to take daily encouragement from God and his word rather than to allow bitterness and anger to destroy her. God encourages widows with his undying love, especially in Isaiah 54:4-5a:

> "Do not be afraid: you will not suffer shame.
>   Do not fear disgrace; you will not be humiliated.
> You will forget the shame of your youth
>   and remember no more the reproach of your widowhood.
> For your Maker is your husband."

It is not known whether or not Anna had children. However, widows who either had no family to support them or had outlived their children usually filled the role of serving in the temple. Then by the time of Christ, the Jews had established a fund for the purpose of taking care of widows and orphans. The widows in return would serve other needy people on behalf of the temple community (Maccabees 3:10, in the Apocrypha). Living through the deaths of your own children is an unbearable sorrow. However, even if this indeed had happened to Anna, she had continually opened her heart and had used her life to serve others. She had allowed God to work his unique surgery— suffering—on her heart to keep her spiritual vision clear:

> And we rejoice in the hope of the glory of God. Not only so, but we also rejoice in our sufferings, because we know that suffering produces perseverance; perseverance, character; and character hope. And hope does not disappoint us, because God has poured out his love into our hearts by the Holy Spirit, whom he has given us" (Romans 5:2b-5).

Character

Anna saturated herself in (Old Testament) prophecies as she stayed in the temple. She lived during a tumultuous time in Jerusalem, but she could see that prophecy was being fulfilled to prepare the way for Christ and his kingdom. The prophet Daniel predicted the coming of the everlasting kingdom of God as he interpreted King Nebuchadnezzar's puzzling dream. God told Daniel that "none of the wicked will understand, but those who are wise will understand" (Daniel 12:8-10).

In the image of a huge statue, the dream predicted three world powers would be built and destroyed before the coming of the kingdom of God. Nebuchadnezzar's Empire (the gold head) was overthrown by the Medo-Persian Empire in 539 B.C. (the silver chest and arms). The next conquering empire, represented by the bronze belly and thighs, was the Greek and Macedonian Empire led by Alexander the Great in 334 B.C. During these world empires, the Jews had no organized political power and remained halfhearted about rebuilding Jerusalem.

In 167 B.C. Antiochus offered a pagan sacrifice, a pig, to honor the Greek god Zeus on the Holy Temple altar. This enraged the Jewish Maccabees family. With their rallied troops, they mounted a full-scale attack and defeated the enemy forces. Jerusalem became self-ruled again. The temple was rededicated and rebuilt in 164 B.C., beginning the Hasmoneon Period in Jerusalem. Only 100 years later, the Roman general Pompey captured Jerusalem. Rome became strong in world conquest (the iron legs in Nebuchadnezzar's dream). Roman world conquests paved the roads on which the future gospel would be spread.

As her long years in the temple continued, Anna's character was being chiseled and refined. God knew that the rebuilding of Jerusalem and the coming of the Christ would encourage Anna, but she did not know when that would happen. She had to wait, hope and trust.

Hope

By the time Anna was around 40 years old, Pompey had captured Jerusalem (62 B.C.) for Rome. Anna knew that God could use wars and hardship, even weak and wicked men to accomplish his ultimate purpose. But at her age, the likelihood of remarriage and a future family, especially under war conditions, seemed impossible. Disappointment again must have tempted her faith. Was it true what others were saying about God? "Look, Jerusalem is defeated; God has forgotten us. There is no Messiah coming."

Her personal life changes in her 50s must have been difficult as the close of childbearing years stood her on the threshold of old age. Anna, however, found great encouragement from God's perspective on the eternal purpose for life. Seeing life through his eyes caused human accomplishments and accumulations to lose their grip on her. Living out God's purpose (Psalm 92:14), she knew she would "bear fruit in old age."

The Jewish king, Herod Antipas, with Rome's approval, began building the temple again in 20 B.C., about the time Anna had her 80th birthday. Herod went to monumental efforts to gain the attention of Rome and the approval of the Jews. His own jealousy of power eventually brought about the death of his wife Marianna, their two sons and later, all the baby boys in Judea at the time of Jesus' birth. Anna could have been frustrated or complacent about another attempt at Jewish spiritual renewal. She had seen so many renewal efforts fail, but she knew the God who ruled the nations (Psalm 67:4).

Anna's faith must have been encouraged when political and historical changes reflected Daniel's prophecy before her eyes. Her soul must have stirred when Zechariah left the temple unable to speak and then spoke again when he named his newborn son, John (Luke 1:5-25, 57-80). Though Anna's old bones experienced sorrow and pain, the expectation of seeing the Messiah kept her alive, vibrant and committed to prayer and fasting. Unlike those around her, Anna was not awed by the physical splendor of Herod's temple, nor was she caught up in the social and political climate of the day. In spite of people's possible opinions of her as a "foolish old woman," she continued her daily, public devotion to God. God thought her worthy, not foolish.

Anna's old friend Simeon also shared her joy. The Lord revealed to him that he would not die before he saw the Lord's Christ. On an "ordinary" day he was moved by the Holy Spirit to enter the temple courts—the same day that Mary and Joseph brought their one-month-old firstborn son, Jesus, to be presented to God in faithfulness to Jewish tradition. Simeon took the baby into his arms and praised God. At that same moment, Anna saw the infant and joined in praise to God. She must have known that Daniel's prophecy was close to fulfillment:

> "In the time of those kings, the God of heaven will set up a kingdom that will never be destroyed, nor will it be left to another people. It will crush all those kingdoms and bring them to an end, but it will itself endure forever. This is the meaning of the vision of the rock cut out of a mountain, but not by human hands—a rock that broke the iron, the bronze, the clay, the silver and the gold to pieces" (Daniel 2:44-45a).

The Longing of a Lifetime Fulfilled

Life can become so painful, burdensome or ordinary that significant moments of life and faith are missed. Yet, Anna's old eyes saw the miracle of the moment. She was given the honor to be the first woman to herald the news that "the Christ child is born." In spite of being over

100 years old,* we find her joyfully crying out in the temple courts, tugging at shirtsleeves, stopping strangers to offer them renewed hope. The hope that had sustained her, now rewarded her.

Herod's enshrined temple existed only 90 years until it was completely destroyed by Titus in 70 A.D. It has never been rebuilt. Anna witnessed and held God enshrined in flesh as a baby, whose kingdom will never be destroyed. God built Anna's long life on her perseverance, character and hope and made her final days triumphant. Surely, not long afterwards, her home was moved from the temple courts to the presence of God.

Just as Daniel prophesied, Jesus, the Messiah, the Rock, struck the fatal blow to the strongest civilization of ancient times and God's eternal kingdom had arrived.

Being God-Centered

The national anthem of most women, "What About Me?" was not Anna's theme song. She lived in a difficult period of history: The spiritual atmosphere was corrupt and the political climate was turbulent. She lived 84 long years as a widow, and possibly a single mother. Yet, she did not accuse God of abusing her "rights," but she honored him and was honored by him.

As a young woman, before I became a disciple, I was overwhelmed and bitter about life. However, all I had to upset me were normal kids, an undisciplined dog, a normal husband and a house to keep. Eventually, I got a clearer picture of my real problem—me. My lack of joy was not due to my externals but my internals: my heart and mind. I clearly remember the day my selfish mind-*set* (and I emphasize "set") loomed large before my eyes. My husband, Roger, was leaving the house for work, and I started rehearsing my self-pity speech again. As he left the house, he kindly but firmly said, "I'm sorry that your day is starting badly, but I have decided that I am going to have a good day."

I was so angry and hurt that I sat down right then and wrote him a letter about how he made me feel. I held nothing back. This letter would be the declaration of my rights. It was perfect!

---

*Luke 2:36 can be translated one of two ways: "she had been a widow for eighty-four years" (NIV footnote and Living Bible) or "[she] was a widow until she was eighty-four."

After I finished my thesis, I re-read it. By about halfway down the page, I was feeling uncomfortable. I picked up a red pen and began circling every "I" and "you." By the time I had reached the end, the letter looked as if it were bleeding to death. "No wonder I am so miserable," I thought, "all I think about is me and my happiness." My heart began to hurt because I was also at a point in my life when I was just beginning to understand Jesus and his unselfish love. Jesus gave up *all* his rights for me so that I could be forgiven. He was not given anything he deserved; instead he was given what he did not deserve: a tortured death. My letter of declaration did eventually led me to freedom. I saw that I was a slave to selfish sin. Repentance freed me up to seek out the forgiveness I desperately needed from God and from those around me.

Anna's lifelong devotion to God also challenges me to embrace getting older as a time of getting stronger and closer to God. One month after being baptized as a true disciple at age 41, a life-threatening cancer was discovered in my uterus. I received radical surgery, radiation treatments and strong medication to combat the cancer. Although it took time to rejoice in my sufferings (Romans 5:2-5), God used the experience to teach me to surrender to him and rely on him for strength.

Anne Morrow Lindbergh, in her book *Gift from the Sea,* describes facing challenges as we age as a time in one's life for shedding shells: shells of ambition, material accumulations, ego, pride, false ambition, masks and armor. "One can at last become oneself." To continue a path of freedom, Anna turned to God with openness and vulnerability and resisted the temptation to hide in a shell of self-focus and self-pity.

God taught me, through physical challenges, to have courage and hope not only for a physical healing, but most of all for spiritual healing. My shells of fear, laziness, selfishness and pride were paralyzing me from serving God the way he deserves. To his glory and credit, 10 years after surgery, I am more thrilled with life's adventures and the joy that comes from "bearing fruit in old age" (Psalm 92:14-15). As Lisa Johnson says it, "Remember, life is not all about you and it is not all about me; it is all about God."

What else would Anna say to us today? As Jesus states,

> "But blessed are your eyes because they see, and your ears because they hear. For I tell you the truth, many prophets and righteous men longed to see what you see but did not see it, and to hear what you hear but did not hear it" (Matthew 13:16-17).

I think Anna would say, "Open your eyes! Be in awe of God and his kingdom today! Be in awe of his Spirit that is living in you!" We are very blessed to be living during this time of unprecedented growth in the modern-day kingdom of God!

Marcia Lamb
Los Angeles, USA

 Are you focused on God and eager to know his will? If God went looking for an Anna today, would he find her in you?

application questions on page 173

4

MARY MAGDALENE
A Woman Repossessed

Matthew 27:55-61; 28:1-11; Mark 15:40-41; 15:46-16:11; Luke 8:1-3; John 19:25; 20:1-18

Demon and *possession* are two ominous words, especially when coupled with each other. A condition referred to in the gospels more than a dozen times, demon-possession was prominent in the miracles and teachings of Jesus.

Historians and scholars are divided in their views of this phenomenon. Some dismiss it as simply a term assigned to the bizarre or inexplicable (like epilepsy, various syndromes or palsies, or insanity). Others speculate that the evil powers in the heavenly realms were in such hysterical turmoil over the implications of the incarnation of God, that hell's fury broke forth on the earth as at no other time in history. Still others believe Satan is always approaching God (as he did with Job) for permission to test and torment people, but God only allows that which serves his eternal purposes. In the ministry of Jesus, demon-possession profoundly served God's purpose to display his Son's power over every existing force, including nature and Satan himself! One grateful recipient of that benevolent power was Mary of Magdala.

◆

She'd been this way for so long; crazy, out of control, hurting herself and everyone around her. She could scarcely remember what it was like to be at peace, free from the dark powers that now dominated her being. This was Mary Magdalene before she met Jesus of Nazareth. Would she ever forget that day? As he looked at her, he seemed to see into the very depths of her being. He saw the pain, the agony, the despair, and he saw Satan in all of his ugliness as his spirits ravaged her soul. The demons resisted him; at the same time they mocked and taunted the Son of God as he stood before them. It only took a few words from Jesus. There was no fanfare or drumroll to advertise the emotional impact of the moment. With a single command Jesus drove out not one, but all seven of the evil spirits that had possessed the life and soul of Mary Magdalene for so long.

Can you imagine the amazement that she felt as the demons fled from her body? It was too good to be true! But there she was, sane and in her right mind. After years of being engulfed in a pit of darkness and despair, she was now basking in the love and light of God.

A Grateful, Devoted Servant

As she looked at Jesus, her heart was filled with a never-ending thankfulness and love. Jesus had done for her what no other person on this earth had been able to do. He had saved her from much more than a physical ailment—he had freed her very soul.

However, the elation she felt must have become tainted as questions about the future came pressing in upon her. Where would she go now? What would she do with this new life of hers? She had nowhere to go, no one else to turn to. And possibly she was afraid, *What if the evil spirits returned?*

Mary Magdalene decided to stay with Jesus and his 12 disciples. She would go where he went, watch him and learn from him, at the same time devoting her life to meeting his needs. Jesus told some to go back home and share with others all they had seen and heard (Legion in Luke 8:26-39). But Jesus allowed Mary to go with them— perhaps out of compassion because she had no one to go home to; perhaps simply because she was special.

Because Mary Magdalene never forgot who she had been or what Jesus had done for her, she would have done anything for Jesus. And certainly she must have reasoned that anything she did to support Jesus' ministry could help someone else like her to experience a similar healing, a similar second chance at life. She had some money, probably an inheritance, that she gladly used to provide for the needs of Jesus and the Twelve. Could she help by gathering food and preparing their meals, by making and washing their clothes, or simply by washing their feet, tired and dirty from the miles of travel? In wholehearted gratitude, she humbly performed all of these services and more, voluntarily becoming Jesus' servant for life.

Deep Friendships

Did I say that Mary was alone, friendless, without a family? She was, but that changed during the months and years she spent with Jesus. You see, there were other women whose lives had been touched by Jesus. Some, like Joanna and Suzanne, who had also been healed of evil spirits and diseases, helped to support the disciples financially. There was another Mary, the mother of two young followers, James and Joses. The ambitious, strong-willed Salome, the mother of James and John, traveled with Jesus as well. Even Jesus' mother, Mary, who at first thought they were all crazy, later became a faithful believer. These were friendships that would last a lifetime—and beyond.

In most of the scriptures referring to Mary Magdalene, we find her with other women. She served Jesus and the other disciples alongside other women, she watched the crucifixion with friends, and when she followed the Twelve to the tomb, she was with "the other Mary" (Matthew 28:1). Two days later, she went to prepare his body for burial along with some of her closest friends, James' mother Mary and Salome. The Mary Magdalene of these passages is far removed from the isolated outcast she was upon her first meeting with Jesus. His friends and family had become her own.

Not only is Mary Magdalene always depicted in the company of friends, but her name is almost always mentioned first. One can't help but wonder: Was she the ringleader, the "make-it-happen" person among the women who followed Jesus? Was she the one who everyone thought of as *the strong one,* the leader?

As far as we know, Mary Magdalene never preached a sermon or taught a class, yet she exemplified what godly leadership is all about. She gave her all to Jesus and inspired others to do the same. Isn't it amazing that a woman whom demons possessed became a model of strength, stability and even leadership?

Devoted to the End

Her wholehearted love and sacrificial devotion never ebbed. Months, and possibly years, later we see her at the cross, overcoming fears for her own safety, eagerly looking for ways to serve the Lord. We see her at his tomb still caring for him, and then we can be sure that she is amidst that group of women praying after Jesus' ascension (Acts 1:14).

Why did love stay so fresh for Mary Magdalene? She never forgot where she was when Jesus found her, and she never stopped being grateful.

Certainly, Mary did not know Jesus very well when she first began to follow him. She knew him because of his reputation and because of the miracle he performed in her life. But it wasn't until she began to follow him that she really came to know and love Jesus. She watched as he got up early and stayed up late every day to spend time in prayer. She saw him tirelessly pouring himself out for the thousands of hungry, sick, empty people who constantly swarmed about him. She heard him teach of the majesty, the love and the judgment of God. The better she knew him, the more deeply she loved and respected him.

Mary Magdalene followed Jesus to the end; she did not turn back even when the soldiers took him to the cross. She took the risk of being identified as one of his followers, hoping that she could do something to make the last hours easier for Jesus. It was a living nightmare to watch Jesus suffer excruciating pain and struggle for every breath. Her ears rang with the mocking voices of the crowds. Her heart broke as she saw Jesus' mother endure the agony of watching her son die like a criminal. Wasn't there something she could do? Mary would stay until the very end. Anything, anything she could do....

When Jesus died on that cross, a part of her own heart must have died also. He was dead and gone, but Mary Magdalene continued to do what she'd always done—care for Jesus' needs. This time she went to the tomb to prepare his dead body for burial. We can only imagine her distress when Jesus' body was gone. Reality came crashing down upon her; Jesus really was gone, dead, and now she didn't even have his body to care for and mourn over.

Standing outside his empty tomb, Mary wept inconsolably. A man approached and asked why she was crying and who she was looking for. Not recognizing him, Mary only cried harder. But then he spoke her name, "Mary"; that wonderful, familiar voice speaking her name in the same, easy way he'd said it so many times before. Instantly, she recognized him. It was Jesus, her teacher and now her Lord! He had risen; he was alive!

We see the love Mary had for Jesus in her grief and in her joyful recognition of his voice. But we also see something else. Of all those who knew and loved him, Jesus appeared *first* to Mary as the resurrected Christ! Jesus deeply loved Mary Magdalene. Her years of sacrifice and service had not gone unnoticed and now, neither did her sorrow.

Jesus had a job to be done, and he went to someone he could count on to do it well—a good and faithful servant. When Mary recognized the risen Lord, he told her, "Go instead to my brothers and tell them, 'I am returning to my Father and your Father, to my God and your God'" (John 20:17). And Mary Magdalene, devoted servant of Jesus, was thrilled to be the one given the privilege of running to the disciples with the wonderful news, "I have seen the Lord!"

Never Be Lacking in Zeal

Spending this last month studying and "living with" Mary Magdalene has been both refreshing and challenging. The fact that she never forgot where she came from has reminded me of where I was when Jesus changed my life. I vividly remember when I was first confronted with real Christianity. Although just a young college student, I knew that the call to follow Jesus wholeheartedly was exactly what I was looking for. That was 25 years ago!

Yet with the passage of years, it is so easy to lose that radical edge, the zeal and joyful exuberance of a new Christian. I have seen countless people become disciples whose lives have been transformed forever. But I have also seen others who became Christians only to lose their love for God because of the challenges and distractions of life. It is easy to become complacent after we get married, overwhelmed when the children arrive, worldly when we acquire money and other possessions, faithless when persecutions come and just plain tired as we get older. Then add some hurts and disappointments, and the growing malignancy of bitterness can invade our lives. I have experienced all of these pulls in my own life and have become increasingly sobered by the schemes of Satan to drag us down and take us out.

I truly believe I have been rescued from the powers of sin and Satan. Yet Mary also forces me to ask myself, *Where am I now? Have I drifted back? Have I allowed any of my past sins to come back and reside in my life again?* The demons of my selfishness, worldliness and weakness are always right at my side, looking for ways to get back in. I have seen more clearly than ever before that I, like Mary Magdalene, must stay very close to Jesus in order to keep them out of my life.

With four children to raise, a ministry to lead, and a large household to run, this feat certainly has not been as simple as it sounds. Not only is it difficult to juggle all of my responsibilities, it is even more challenging to stay spiritually focused and close to God. For some reason, we tend to believe that life will become easier as we grow older. As one who has experienced a lot of life, I have realized: It doesn't! Life has become more demanding and challenging as the years have gone by, and my faith and dependence on God have had to either increase proportionately or risk being lost completely. This means I have to work diligently to keep the Jesus of the Bible real in my own heart and life. I pray every day to be able to see the miraculous power of God working, just as I did when I was a young Christian. It takes effort to keep my relationship with God fresh and alive.

In addition to staying close to God, I have also relied on spiritual women in my life to help me remain focused and keep a soft heart. The busier life gets, the easier it becomes to drift from the people we need the most. Just like Mary, I need other women in my life. I need them for their help and advice, but even more so for the strength that comes from their companionship and friendship. Nothing can replace friendships that remain close through the years and experiences of life. I am reminded of a song that I learned as a child, "Make new friends but keep the old. One is silver and the other is gold."

Mary Magdalene exemplified all of these things. Her life and devotion to Jesus stand as a testimony to me and all other women that we too can make it all the way, to the very end!

Geri Laing
Chapel Hill, North Carolina, USA

 FOCUS Although demon-possession may not be experienced in the same way today as in New Testament times, the pull of Satan in our lives is still very real. What are the "demons" that seek to control your life? How can Jesus set you free from these?

application questions on page 174

5

HERODIAS
She Did It Her Way

Matthew 14:1-12; Mark 6:14-29; Luke 3:19-20

The family tree of the Herods bore only rotten fruit. Their hunger for power and thirst for blood ran chills down the spines of those in Palestine. Godless and self-serving, they were known for unrestrained treachery and cruelty. Herod the Great was the root of the tree—a root which tapped into the blood of the deposed Macabee family. When threatened by a new king, one to be born in Bethlehem of Judea, he had all the baby boys killed. Herod Antipas, a king "wanna be," beheaded John the Baptist; and Herod Agrippa I was the first persecutor of the church and the one who beheaded James.

One of the female branches of this family tree was Herodias. Her name was simply a feminine form of the royal family name of Herod, and her character was undeniably a feminine form of that of her godless male predecessors.

◆

What can we learn from a woman who was married to one man and yet would stop at nothing to become the wife of her husband's brother? What can we learn from a woman who, when confronted by a prophet of God, resisted and rebelled against him and his teaching? What can we learn from a woman who pushed her husband to act against his own conscience? What can we learn from a woman who urged her own daughter to rush into evil? What can we learn from a woman who was responsible for the death of a prophet of God? We can, and must, learn a lot about sins that can destroy us as women, wives and mothers.

Her Way or No Way

Herodias was a selfishly ambitious woman. She had her idea of the way that she wanted her life to be, and she would stop at nothing to get what she wanted. She was greedy, arrogant, manipulative, rash and bitter. I see in her a woman so caught up in her own passions and schemes that she is completely oblivious to the eternal harm that she is inflicting on those around her. As we look more closely at her sin and the consequences of her sin, remember that God is appealing to us through his word to let go of the ways that seem right to us and learn to do things his way (Proverbs 14:12).

Herodias was not content with the man she had chosen to marry. Philip probably didn't have as much power and money as his brother Herod. And Herodias wanted more!

Greed (material or otherwise), lust and a lack of contentment are sins that must be openly acknowledged and confessed. Women through the ages have become obsessed by thoughts of things that they did not have: a boyfriend, a husband, some material possession, a certain role in life or in the kingdom. Paul wrote to the Philippians that he had "learned to be content whatever the circumstances" (Philippians 4:11). And that is good news: Contentment is not natural! It is something that must be learned. It certainly was not natural to Herodias, and it is clear that she had no desire to learn it. What is natural is whining, complaining and competitive attitudes that tempt and bombard people every day. Through openness, prayer and advice, disciples can overcome the greed in their lives and learn to be content. This was not an option that Herodias opened herself up to; therefore, greed and discontent were her constant companions.

A Chance to Change

God, in his mercy, sends life-giving challenges and rebukes to people of all ages (Proverbs 15:31). He sent his message to Herodias through the courage of a great prophet. God through John gave her the chance to see her sin and to repent. In her arrogance she refused to change. Herodias simply was not listening. Her own agenda remained foremost in her mind.

I deeply believe that God disciplines because he loves (Hebrews 12:5-6). How challenging it is to accept discipline at times—especially when it comes, as it often does, through another person. Imagine this unkempt, desert-man daring to confront finely groomed Herodias with her sin. Imagine her, standing tall, chin tilted upward, with obvious disdain in her eyes, refusing to break or to be deterred from having her way. Herodias' pride destroyed her and her family. How true it is that "God opposes the proud but gives grace to the humble" (James 4:6).

Unleashed Resentment

Herod's reaction to John the Baptist was somewhat different than his wife's reaction. The Bible tells us that "Herod feared John and protected him, knowing him to be a righteous and holy man" and that when "Herod heard John, he was greatly puzzled; yet he liked to listen to him" (Mark 6:20). Herodias wanted him killed, but she was unable to persuade her husband to do things her way. Instead of submitting to her husband's decision to simply imprison John or allowing her husband's curiosity about John to influence her, she continued to scheme and wait for the opportunity to destroy God's prophet. Resentment seethed in her heart, eager for an outlet.

On the day of the banquet she manipulated the circumstances, and she manipulated her husband, much to his distress—she got what she wanted. In Proverbs 6:18 we learn that God hates "a heart that devises wicked schemes." Her mind and her heart were not even close to being devoted to bringing her husband good, and not harm, each and every day (Proverbs 31:12). Rather than being the "worthy woman," she was the epitome of the "unworthy woman."

Perhaps the saddest element in the account of Herodias is her behavior as a mother. When her trusting, admiring daughter turns to her for advice, she "prompts" (Matthew 14:8) her daughter to join with her in committing a terrible sin. She uses her daughter as a means to satisfy her own wicked desires without any concern as to the consequences this act will have in her daughter's life. One would certainly expect that the dance performed by the daughter was sensual in nature, motivating Herod through his lust to make a rash promise. Not only was Herodias an immoral woman herself; she had raised a daughter who was just like her through and through.

What was it in the heart of Herodias that drove her to commit these sins? Bitterness. The Bible tells us that Herodias "nursed a grudge against John and wanted to kill him" (Mark 6:19). Bitterness. Nursing a grudge. Unconfessed bad attitudes. Festering quiet reservations. No wonder God commands his children to "get rid of all bitterness, rage and anger" (Ephesians 4:31). Herodias was so consumed by bitterness that she was responsible for a murder!

Bitterness destroys people from the inside out. It wears them down and steals their hope of change. Only with God can anyone be freed from the soul-killing clenches of this sin. God desires to forgive people for the pain they have inflicted on both themselves and on others.

Acceptance of God's forgiveness frees people to be strong enough to forgive those who have caused them pain (Colossians 3:13).

Imagine what an incredible sense of satisfaction and power Herodias must have felt as her daughter handed her the tray with the head of John the Baptist on it. But in spite of the fact that Herodias "got her way," God won, as always, the ultimate victory! Herodias may have been able to destroy John's body and to silence his tongue, but she could not kill his soul (Matthew 10:28). God brought John home to be with him for eternity!

But for the Grace of God

I am very grateful to have been asked to study and write about Herodias, because I do not think I would have ever meditated on the scriptures that tell us her story. I am not drawn to her. I do not want to be like her. I found myself wanting to look down on her and judge her and distance myself from her. However, the more I prayed about her, the more I realized that, without God, I could easily become exactly like her. And this realization was both challenging and faith building.

It is always challenging to re-examine our hearts and strive to identify the sins that we need to confess and overcome. What I see in Herodias is a woman whose life and character were defined by years of unrecognized, unconfessed and undealt-with sin. The question that I asked myself as I examined Herodias' sin was, "How far will I let myself go before I confess my sin and get the encouragement that I need?"

The Hebrew writer tells us that we need daily encouragement in order to keep our hearts pure and soft (Hebrews 3:12-13). Satan, however, lies to us and tells us that we were not really complaining; we were being open. He tells us that all wives try to get their own way sometimes and that all mothers lose their patience with their children. We hear him tell us that our last little outburst was not really that bad. He leads us to believe that we have the right to hold on to our anger because after all, so-and-so really did do such-and-such to us. He slowly and insidiously convinces us to lower our expectations for righteousness and compromise our integrity. When we listen to Satan, keep these things inside and try to deal with them ourselves, we become blind to the consequences of our sin in our own lives and families.

I was challenged by the thought that the sins that led Herodias to commit murder are the same sins that Satan tempts me with every day. And I know that I never want to end up like her! This study led me to recommit myself to Jesus' standard for daily righteousness!

I also felt challenged to find that there was a little bit of a Pharisee in me. My first reaction to Herodias was to look down on her and to be thankful that I was nothing like her. These thoughts were particularly present in my reaction to her as a mother as I thought, *How could she do that to her own daughter?* It was to people who had this same kind of reaction to others that Jesus told the Parable of the Pharisee and the Tax Collector in Luke 18:9-14. My reaction should have been, "God, have mercy on me, a sinner, and help me not to give in to these sins that I see in Herodias." This reaction would have led me to have compassion on Herodias and not to judge her.

It is so important to examine our reactions to the people around us. Recently, I was sitting at lunch with a group of disciples, and we were discussing the upcoming wedding of one of the women in our congregation. The only member of the bride's entire family who will be present at her wedding is her sister. Her parents, who are strongly against the church, sent a letter and copies of articles against the church to those that they knew received a wedding invitation. One of the disciples, during the course of our conversation about how to strengthen and encourage this sister, said, "How could people do this to their own daughter?" I remembered the question that I had asked myself about Herodias, and I shared her story with the sisters. Although we were tempted to judge these parents harshly, God reminded us that we could end up just as hard and confused as they are if we don't remain thankful for God's grace and deal seriously with our sin every day.

As always, this study of God's word greatly increased my faith and gratitude (Romans 10:17). I was reminded that I have now, and will always have, a relationship with God as my source of contentment! (1 Timothy 6:6-10). I am thankful to know many disciples who love me and are willing to speak the truth to me, in love (Ephesians 4:15), so that I will never remain blinded by my pride. As a wife and mother,

I am deeply grateful to have God's word to guide me and to be in God's kingdom, surrounded by godly women who set an example for me and can train me in these areas of my life (Titus 2:3-5). And then there is the miracle of repentance and forgiveness! God gives us the freedom to live our lives in such a way that we will never be burdened by regret! (2 Corinthians 7:10). Every day is a new beginning, a fresh opportunity to live righteously for God! God has given us everything we need for life and godliness.

What about the *Herodiases* of the world? There are so many women who live as she lived. They are fighting to get their own way, and they are in pain and causing pain in the lives of those around them. My prayer is that we will not have a judgmental, self-righteous attitude toward them, but have compassion on them and strive to show them God's way, motivated by the thought: There, but for the grace of God, go I.

Adrienne Scanlon
Paris, France

In everything we do, as disciples, we have an opportunity to influence our families and our friends. Are you taking seriously the impact that you have as you are or are not manipulative in order to get your own way?

application questions on page 174

6

SINFUL WOMAN
An Outpouring of Faith

Luke 7:36-50

The Roman custom of reclining at table had reached Palestine, at least among the wealthy. Dinner was an elaborate and lengthy ritual. A typical dinner party consisted of nine or less guests who were each assigned one or two servants. The servant who greeted the guests at the door would remove their shoes, bathe their feet, and offer clean sandals before escorting them to their places at the table. After the guests reclined on couches positioned around a horseshoe-shaped table, the servant would remove the sandals and bring water for hand washing.

There were generally three courses, and because eating was done with the fingers, the servants brought fresh basins of water between each course to wash again. This meal generally lasted three or more hours. To say that the guests felt important and pampered is an understatement.

A Pharisee hosting a dinner would have been fastidious in prohibiting unclean food at his table (any food ritually unfit for Jewish consumption). He would have been equally cautious to exclude any unclean person. An unescorted, uninvited, unclean woman would certainly not have been welcomed.

◆

She was a nameless prostitute in a nameless town in the first century. She had "lived a sinful life in that town," which leaves an impression of one no longer young and resilient, but used, and on the bitter side of experience. She learned that Jesus was eating at a Pharisee's house locally, and she made an amazingly unorthodox decision: The lady of the night would crash the religious leader's exclusive kosher dinner party, unclean and uninvited. What could she possibly have been thinking?

Your Sins Are Forgiven

One fact is clear and certain: she *needed* to be with Jesus. She needed to touch Jesus. She loved Jesus, very much—Jesus himself said she did (Luke 7:47). She likely stopped at the brothel where she lived and picked up an alabaster jar of perfume, most certainly a tool of her trade. At some point as she made her way across town, she began to cry, a few trickling tears that turned into sobs—still, she hurried on. Was she so *certain* that Jesus would receive her? The reaction that might meet her when she got there didn't even seem to matter—the only important thing was to get there, to be where Jesus was.

At some point in this woman's life, she became irrevocably convinced of two things: one, that she was living a wretched life without hope; and two, that Jesus was exactly who he said he was: the only Son of the living God. Pure. Perfect. Able and willing to forgive all her sins. Her personal Messiah? Overwhelming. Too good to be true.

Amazing news had reached her ears—perhaps overheard in the town's market square—that a carpenter from Nazareth had simply ordered an evil spirit out of a man one Sabbath day in a synagogue in Capernaum (Luke 4:31-37). Then came the rumors that this same carpenter willingly touched and healed a leper (Luke 5:12-15). He healed paralytics, she heard, and he promised the forgiveness of all their sins. It must have thrilled her to hear not only of these miracles, but to hear the accounts of how Jesus exasperated the Pharisees and teachers of the Law, her tormentors (Luke 5:17-31).

The picture she was getting of Jesus must have been a bit like a superhero/rebel, coming out of nowhere to be the most talked about personality of her day—reputed to be a prophet and religious teacher, yet breaking all the molds and defying the established laws of the Sabbath and the Pharisees' tedious traditions. She fell in love with this Jesus.

More than likely, she was present in the crowd of people who heard him preach on different occasions, and her own heart was convicted of all its worldliness and sin. At the same time, God must have reawakened a dream in her through Jesus' message of forgiveness—an impossible dream of restored innocence, of starting over, of a life with depth and meaning. She knew then exactly who she was, and she knew exactly who Jesus was. She desperately needed her sins forgiven, and she knew that Jesus was her only hope.

Your Faith Has Saved You

Hebrews 11:6 describes faith as not only believing that God exists but that he rewards those who earnestly seek him. Faith is focusing on God and trusting him. The sinful woman had this kind of faith that pleases God.

What must she have looked like to Simon the Pharisee and his distinguished guests as she burst through the door unannounced and stood behind Jesus as he reclined at the table? Many of us are uncomfortable to shed a tear in public—she was weeping so much that she literally soaked Jesus' feet. She fell to her knees and with disheveled, unbound hair, wiped his feet and kissed them—which was surely a lowly and absolutely tasteless act in the eyes of the company gathered.

The perfume she poured and the clothes she wore betrayed her profession. She was a pathetic sight. Had she been concerned about how she looked or what kind of impression she made on these people, she would never have touched the Lord that night. The only thing that mattered to her was getting to Jesus.

Simon the Pharisee surveyed the damage to the atmosphere of his dinner party, cool and aloof. Jesus interrupted his thoughts to tell him the parable of the moneylender and two debtors who could not pay. What was it like to be in debt for a year-and-a-half's wages, or even a month-and-a-half's wages, to a first-century moneylender? There were no First World banks as we know them. It was probably much like 1990s Russia, where "moneylenders" equals Mafia. Owing almost any sum of money to them rapidly becomes an issue of life and death. Even a debt of 50-days' wages is impossible to repay because of interest rates. In just a couple of months, the sum of your initial debt goes rocketing hopelessly out of reach.

By telling this story, Jesus was putting Simon and the prostitute on exactly the same level—neither could ever hope to repay God for the debt of sin they each had incurred. The penalty for this predicament? You lose your life. But Simon was oblivious to this, and in his religious self-righteousness—faithless.

The difference between the two of them is striking, the one with real faith and the one with "religious" faith. The Pharisee foolishly thought paying back any debt of his was within his means. Overconfident of his position and relationship to God, he didn't even extend to Jesus the basic courtesies one might expect from a host. "You did not give me any water for my feet…You did not give me a kiss…You did not put oil on my head…" (Luke 7:44-46). Basically, Jesus is saying to Simon, *You figure your debt is not so serious* ("he who has been forgiven little," Luke 7:47); *you don't need me, therefore you don't love me very much.* But the prostitute, the faithful one, not only gave Jesus water for his feet, but gave the most precious water imaginable—real tears from the depths of her soul. She not only gave Jesus a kiss, but groveled at his feet in sincere self-abasement and lavished the dirtiest and lowliest part of his body with kisses. She did not put oil on his head, but in wiping his feet clean with her own hair and pouring expensive perfume on them, she gave above and beyond what was expected. She saw her need, and with incredible sincerity and desperation, expressed it in faith to the One who could save her.

Go in Peace

It was the moment of a miracle. When she rose from the floor and left that room, she was changed for all time. She touched God— the honesty and grittiness of a prostitute triumphed over the pomp and propriety of a Pharisee. Of all the women in history, she surely was one of the most blessed! She had a dream that meant more to her than anything else in the world, and against incredible odds, it came true. God in the flesh looked into her eyes—directly. Spoke to her—personally.

Because she was so honest, she witnessed firsthand the heart that we struggle so much to understand. She was in terrible shape, and she admitted it. As a result, she'd never again doubt God's love for her or his acceptance of her. She was open when she was at her absolute worst and, in that condition, received God's unconditional love and acceptance. She became a secure and fulfilled woman because she dared to be herself.

Get Real

One of the most disturbing things for me about studying this passage for the last several weeks has been confronting myself with the fact that if I had been in her place, I would never have gone to

Simon's house; I would never have seen or touched the Lord in person; I would *never* have heard him speak personally to me; I would not have had my sins forgiven, been saved, been told I had faith or gotten my name in the Bible. I would have missed the opportunity of the ages—why? *Because I wasn't invited to the party. Because Jesus needs to talk about important things with Simon and I'd be intruding. Because I don't have time to change out of my prostitute clothes. Because the bodyguards would throw me out anyway before I got in.* Because in my human nature I'm so concerned with how things look on the outside and how other people view me. Acting within all the right parameters, I'd have been paralyzed and would have missed the miracle.

I have been so inspired by this first-century prostitute who touched God! She was so much more honest than I am, had more integrity than I have—she sinned loudly and visibly, and repented dramatically. In contrast to her, during my own period of sexual promiscuity before I became a disciple, I did everything to keep it a secret from everybody. I even stood in the middle of my bedroom once and tried to convince myself that my one-night stand didn't actually happen. I couldn't reconcile my image of myself with what I had done.

As a young Christian I was a people-pleaser to the max. Conflict avoider. Truth distorter. What a colossal waste of energy! And as you might guess, not a very effective fisher of women. I don't believe that even one woman remained faithful in the kingdom as a result of my efforts during my first two years as a disciple.

The beautiful thing about this sinful woman is that she didn't waste time trying to be something she wasn't. She was a mess. She was flat-out desperate. And so am I, even after nine years as a Christian. The moment I forget that, I'm back in my fruitless and faithless young Christian days. The sins I commit every day now—be it lack of faith in not persevering in evangelism, or responding defensively to my husband—are no less offensive than the ones I confessed before my baptism. This realization should send me running to Jesus in my quiet times with the urgency of this woman in Luke 7—and with the same assurance of total acceptance, peace and blessed change!

Sadly, many of us have unstable and insecure relationships with God because we haven't learned the sinful woman's lesson. We've got to get real and admit our failures every day, loudly, instead of stressing out trying to convince ourselves we're really not doing that badly. *If we don't confess much, we don't feel forgiven much.* If we don't face the fear of being open, we never get free of it. Through Jesus, God has spoken these very same words to every one who is a disciple. Let's get up from our knees every day trusting God and believing the promises: *Your many sins are forgiven! Your faith has saved you! Go in peace.*

Tammy Fleming
Moscow, Russia

 Is there anything on your conscience you know you should confess? Are you putting it off because you are afraid? Confess it today!

application questions on page 175

7

BLEEDING WOMAN
The Touch of Faith

Matthew 9:18-22; Mark 5:21-34; Luke 8:40-48

"Rabbi, who sinned, this man or his parents, that he was born blind?" (John 9:2). The question posed to Jesus by his disciples was reflective of cultural belief: The afflicted are cursed by God. When the affliction itself was considered unclean, as in leprosy or prolonged vaginal bleeding, the sufferer was treated with double contempt. In the case of vaginal bleeding, the law of Moses stated the following:

> When a woman has a discharge of blood for many days at a time other than her monthly period or has a discharge that continues beyond her period, she will be unclean as long as she has the discharge, just as in the days of her period (Leviticus 15:25).

Medicine was surprisingly advanced in New Testament times, and afflicted people sought the help of physicians. The famous Greek doctor Hippocrates (460-377 B.C.) had done much research in herbal cures and physiology and had written the oath of integrity taken by doctors even today. The fact that surgery was relatively common is incredible since synthetic medicines like antibiotics and anesthetics were not yet discovered. Amputation, tracheotomy and Cesarean section (named after Julius Caesar who was thus delivered) were among the recorded procedures. Although first-century doctors were appreciated and respected, they obviously, even more than today, could not solve every problem.

◆

"If I just touch his clothes, I will be healed" (Mark 5:28).

Have you ever wanted something really badly? To be accepted at a certain school? To win a contest? To pass a test? To marry the person you love? To buy a house? To have children? Have you ever thought that if you could just *do* this thing or *have* this thing, your life would be happy and complete?

Faith to Reach

The woman in Mark 5 had just such a driving desire—it was to be healed. Imagine that *you* are this woman. You have dealt with a continual flow of vaginal blood for 12 years. You have seen many doctors, but instead of getting better, you are getting worse. Instead of lessening, the flow is increasing. You are humiliated by having exposed yourself to doctor after doctor—all men. In Jewish society, you are not only recognized as sick but also as *unclean* because of the strict sanitation regulations. Probably the news has spread around town about your being unclean. Since anyone you touch becomes ceremonially unclean, people draw back from you as you pass. All your relationships have been cut off or distanced because of your illness. Accompanying the social and emotional ostracism, you are anemic and weakened because of blood loss. This would be hard for anyone to have to live through.

Despite all these obstacles in her life, this woman *did not lose faith* in God's power to heal her. When she encountered Jesus amidst a crowd of people, hope was still alive in her heart. The very fact that she had gone to many doctors over those 12 years shows her determination to get well. Moreover, her faith was so strong that she thought that merely touching the hem of Jesus' cloak could heal her.

She did not allow past failures to cause her to give up or to become cynical. How easy it would have been to have squashed the hope rising in her heart. Faith said, *Move forward. Trust. This man truly is of God.* What started out as a desperate thought became her victory because she believed in the power of God.

Courage to Touch

This afflicted woman's efforts are not only indicative of her faith, but of her courage as well. She was brave enough to approach Jesus even as he was being summoned by Jairus, the well-connected, influential synagogue ruler. His 12-year-old daughter was close to death, and he was urgent about Jesus getting to her quickly. For every year the girl had lived, this woman had bled. She so much wanted to have a normal life. But even in her deep desire, it would have been so easy for her to stop right there, just a few feet away from realizing her dream. She could have told herself, *This girl living is more important than your being healed. Don't try to touch him. It might distract him.* But she kept her focus. *Just touch him. Something will happen. Just reach out and touch him. Don't let anything stop you now that you are this close.* Through the crowd she pressed, defying the religious laws by touching person after person. Over, under, around the people she reached—no easy feat.

She felt the brush of the cloth on her fingertips. Miracle of miracles! What no doctor had been able to do, Jesus did in passing. What a moment it must have been when she felt the bleeding stop! No more pain! No more suffering! No more doctors! No more rejection from society! No more discouragements about her health! She was healed! Yet, she could not just go away after that because the Lord felt her touch him! "At once, Jesus realized that power had gone out from him. He turned around in the crowd and asked, 'Who touched my clothes?'" (Mark 5:30). The woman tried to go unnoticed, but "Jesus kept looking around to see who had done it" (Mark 5:32). She was afraid but told Jesus what had happened to her. It did not matter if she got scolded—she was healed. She had to say something.

Her faith gave her courage to overcome her fears and her past discouragements. She was brave enough to go to Jesus to touch him, but she also dared to speak to him. She did not want to bother Jesus, but there was no avoiding it because her faith had drawn power from him. In the end Jesus wanted to recognize this courageous woman's faith.

She was unafraid to try something new—to reach out for a power she did not understand. She heard a man with a heart-changing message, and she saw the life-changing effect that he had on the people around him. She could have been just a face in the crowd that day—one of hundreds who went home having seen the Son of God from a distance. But she had the faith and the courage to go against the crowd. She reached out and received power from the God of the universe through the hem of homespun cloth. Praise God that he compassionately responds to the humble faith of hurting people.

How Much Do You Want It?

Before I became a Christian, one of my greatest sins was a lack of trust. Growing up in New York City, I can say most confidently, did not inspire me to trust people. This one sin became the root of all my sins. I became prideful, closed, aloof and very superficial. As a non-Christian, I looked sweet on the outside, but no one really knew what was inside. When I became a Christian, I was challenged about my sin. I was told that if I did not change, I would never be effective as a disciple. Over and over again, I would fall into the same distrust no matter how hard I tried. As a result of my sin, some people had not become Christians and others had fallen away. When I realized the eternal effect my sin was having on others, I decided with urgency that I would change and deal with this area in my life decisively.

I prayed to God that he would do whatever he needed to do in my life to cause me to depend on him totally. God did not delay in answering that prayer! My husband and other leaders in my life helped me to get in touch with and resolve my distrust. As I repented, God helped me to trust him and the people he put in my life to encourage and challenge me. Whatever was left of self-sufficiency and lack of trust is being cleansed through my experience with a chronic disease (lupus) I contracted several years ago. All my life I disliked depending on others, but God has humbled me and shown me that I need people in my life.

The result of prayer and of determination is that I now trust God more deeply than ever. With the difficulties, I have not come to love God *less,* but I have come to adore him *more and more* as he cares for me and meets my needs. I continually see God's power working in my life. I now have a reverent fear of God, not in a *fearful* way but rather in *awe* of his great strength!

It can be so easy to give up and become hopeless in hard times. But God provides people like the bleeding woman in the Bible to inspire us to persevere and to always have faith. The challenge is to never stop short of the goal—to be with our Lord Jesus forever. We must reach out daily and touch the hem of his garment. We never need to watch him from a distance. The promise is that as we reach out for him, "he is not far from each one of us" (Acts 17:27). Don't allow anything to keep you from reaching out to Jesus!

Erica Kim
Tokyo, Japan

 FOCUS

How determined are you to grow in your weakest area? How open are you being with others who can help you change?

application questions on page 176

8

THE WIDOW OF NAIN
God's Specialty: The Impossible

Luke 7:11-17

In preparation for burial, the body of the deceased was anointed with ointments and spices. Afterward, a funeral procession would carry the body on a bier or in a coffin to the place of burial, outside the city. Cremation was denounced as a heathen practice; whereas the Jewish people showed great respect for the dead body. It was considered unlawful to walk irreverently, to eat, drink or read among where the dead were buried. In Galilee the women preceded the bier or casket in processions, because it was said of women in an ancient Jewish commentary that they ushered death into the world, so they should be the first in the funeral procession. It was just such a procession that Jesus came upon outside of the city of Nain.*

◆

The brightness of the morning's first rays of sunlight awakened her. As her eyes adjusted to the light, her mind had to adjust to reality. What a contrast to the brightness of the day—the heaviness and darkness of her reality—just yesterday the fever that her son had been fighting overcame him, and he died. Today she was to bury her only son. These feelings were all too familiar and weighed on her doubly as she remembered burying her beloved husband. She had wondered then how she could endure such a loss, but also knew she had to be strong for her young son. She could almost feel the comfort of his arms as they held on to each other at her husband's burial; and even in that memory her present pain and emptiness seemed greater than ever! How could this be happening? Again? This son was the last of her family; he had become her sole support—he was all she had!

Friends were around her. She was up, dressed and had eaten—when? how? what? Again she remembered: Routine things become a blur at times like this. How much she needed these friends who had been with her through the years in her little hometown of Nain. How grateful she felt in the midst of her deep grief as she saw the crowd gathering outside to be with her.

---

*Alfred Edersheim. *Sketches of Jewish Social Life* (Peabody, Massachusetts: Hendrickson Publishers, 1994) 155-156.

As soon as the professional mourners arrived, the funeral procession began. The wailing women led the way; the bier holding the body of her precious son was being carried by four young men who were his close friends. She touched the tapestry covering the bier in a futile attempt to somehow connect one final time with her son, then stepped back to walk behind it. She had held back her tears for awhile, but suddenly felt their surge surfacing uncontrollably. The arms of her friends supported and comforted her as they walked along, yet she could not stop weeping.

Since her eyes were blinded by tears, she had not noticed a man walking toward her as they neared the town gate. She was startled when the man said, "Don't cry!"; others had sympathetically said the same words, but his words had a sense of command surrounded by compassion that moved her. Immediately she stopped crying, and only then saw the crowd of people with him—for an instant she was puzzled that he would leave the crowd of his own followers to come tell her not to cry. Then she was even more amazed as she watched him walk past her and touch the coffin in which her son's body lay.

Those carrying the coffin stood still; the funeral procession stopped and the crowd was hushed, since the wailing women had also obeyed the man's words. Then Jesus spoke words to her son that she would never forget, "Young man, I say to you, get up!" And the young man did! Incredible! No one had ever seen a dead man raised to life! The young man immediately started talking—asking questions—trying to understand what had happened. With the crowd pressing in around them, Jesus had to make way for the young man's mother to get to him. What a reunion! His arms were again around her to comfort and support her. Again her tears flowed uncontrollably, but these tears were tears of joy and thankfulness.

Getting Out of God's Way

How easy it would have been for this grieving widow to look at the complete stranger and say to him, "Who do you think you are to tell me not to cry? What do you know of pain and loss?" As a woman, she could have held on to her emotional side, her need to express all her feelings, her inability to control the raging grief within her. From her viewpoint she had every right to resent and resist this man— surely insensitive and unaware of all her circumstances—breaking into this personal, private moment of intense suffering.

But…she did not! In a true sense she got out of Jesus' way and let him do his work. She obeyed and stopped crying, and by her obedience acknowledged his authority. She did not draw any lines to limit Jesus and so relinquished her control to him. By getting out of God's way, the widow of Nain experienced the incredible miracle of seeing life restored to her dead son.

Praise God

The end result of this unimaginable event was that all the people were filled with awe and praised God. The people said, "A great prophet has appeared among us. God has come to help his people" (Luke 7:16). The widow of Nain and her son were forever changed—impacted for the rest of their lives by the touch of Jesus. They would not miss an opportunity to powerfully share their testimony of life restored, as this news about Jesus spread throughout the country.

The work of God is often displayed through hardship and suffering. The widow of Nain simply got out of God's way so that he could accomplish his specialty—the impossible! The focal point was not the widow or her son, but Jesus and who he is! Then praise and thanks were given to God honoring him and spreading his good news to others.

Healing the Hurt

Unlike the widow of Nain, many of us have lived lives relatively free of hardship. When I was younger, I didn't think about bad things happening to me. I had lived a sheltered life. God knew I needed some character building (Romans 5:3-5). After Al and I had been married for a couple of years, we were thrilled to surprise our parents with the news that they were to be grandparents. All went very well in my pregnancy until, seven weeks before my due date, I went into labor and delivered a baby boy, Gary Todd, weighing 4 lbs.,10 oz. He immediately had breathing problems, and after struggling for three days, he died.

We were heartbroken and sad, having to plan our baby's funeral instead of celebrating his birth. I remember realizing that we were vulnerable—hard things can happen to us. Through our tears we asked "Why?" but we didn't get an answer. I wondered if God were punishing us, but we held on to his love for us. It was a very hard time, yet we felt God's comfort and strength like never before, as well as the support and love from family and friends. We had to wrestle with accepting God's will when it was not at all what we wanted. We chose to trust God through our hurt and to hold on to each other, more deeply bonded than ever.

What a happy day it was for us about a year later when God blessed us with a healthy baby girl, Staci Leigh. She was born five weeks early with no problems. We had waited an extra long time for her, so she was a special delight to us.

Two years later I was pregnant again. The doctor was watching me closely to try to detect any signs of premature labor. At my check-up between six and seven months I was already dilated a little, so the doctor sent me to the hospital for corrective surgery to put a permanent tie around the cervix. (That would mean subsequent deliveries would be Cesarean.) Shortly before the scheduled surgery, I went into labor which could not be stopped. In a few hours, much to our surprise, I delivered twin girls, Laura and Lisa, each weighing slightly more than two pounds. The excitement at the birth of our twin girls was short lived. They, too, had breathing problems, in addition to the other complications of premature birth, and only lived about twenty-four hours. Again we were coping with loss, and this time after the initial excitement of twins.

As I thought about the widow of Nain experiencing such a major loss, again I recalled some of my feelings. After we had lost our son, I thought we had had our share. Surely we were "refined." I began to see that God doesn't measure things the way we do. Life is not about score keeping—adding up points for losses and gains. God is working in us individually and uniquely to mold and shape our characters. And that is not a one-experience job!

We remembered our Source of strength when we lost our son and again marveled at the way God supplies his strength just when it is needed. In much the way the widow must have been comforted by her son's presence when she lost her husband, we were comforted by having Staci when we lost the twins. At times when I felt the grief the most, I wondered how other people could go on laughing, shopping, etc., when my world had come to such an abrupt halt. Having another child around me forced me to go on with day-to-day life and also helped to fill the emptiness we felt from our losses.

Just as there was a crowd of friends around the widow at the death of her son, we had our family and many friends who helped us and showered love on us. I don't remember much about what people said to us during those times, but I do remember people being there with us. That has helped me to realize that I don't have to know exactly the "right" words to say to someone who is hurting, but my presence can make a great difference. I also realized that life quickly goes on for other people. After a few weeks my loss was not felt much by others. It was my choice whether I would get up and go forward or sit and cry over our losses; but I knew that if I chose the latter, I would find myself alone much of the time. Holding on to God's love and promises, as well as being open about my feelings, made it possible to go forward.

After a few months I had the corrective surgery that had been canceled when I went into labor with the twins. Soon after that I got pregnant again. Kristi Deanne was safely delivered—although it was an emergency C-section four weeks early! We grew more and more grateful for healthy babies.

God's healing is amazing and as time goes by, the pain of hurts and losses is softened through his power. Al and I still wanted to have another child, so after a couple of years we decided to try one more time. Again God blessed me with a very healthy pregnancy...again I went into labor five weeks early...again I had an emergency C-section...and again we were blessed with a baby girl, Keri Lynne! But at two days old, Keri began to have breathing problems severe enough that the doctors wanted her transferred to another hospital for more specialized treatment.

This was the pinnacle of my wrestling with God. With clenched fists and tears I cried out, "No! No! No! This can't be happening again! I can't go through this again! We can't take another loss!" It seemed so hopeless since we had lost all of the babies who had breathing trouble. Surely the widow of Nain must have felt similar emotions as her son got weaker and weaker. The facts looked so bleak and dark that it was hard to have hope. Then Jesus steps in and says, "Don't cry!"

As I poured out my heart to God, he helped me remember his strength that had come just when I needed it. With that realization I was able to surrender Keri to him, acknowledging that whatever happened, God had gotten us through it before and he would get us through it again. I learned later that at nearly the same time I surrendered, Keri made a pronounced change for the good while on the ambulance ride to the other hospital—enough so that on her arrival the doctors wondered why she had been brought there. Needless to say, we felt much like the widow of Nain—that Jesus' "touch" had restored life to our child!

As God continues to mold and shape our lives, he intends for us to share with others the lessons he teaches us. We have had many opportunities to help and comfort others with the same comfort that we received (2 Corinthians 1), but we had to apply the lessons again personally when our daughter Keri and her husband, Steve, were expecting their first baby. In her seventh month Keri noticed that the baby was not moving; an ultrasound revealed that their baby boy was dead.

How devastatingly helpless we felt! It was one thing to go through the losses ourselves; it was quite another challenge to see our children hurt. The reality of God's power was so evident as he strengthened Keri and Steve through the delivery of their stillborn son. It was so obvious that God was giving them the same comfort and help he had given us. Our common experiences bonded us and made us closer. They knew firsthand that God had brought us through similar trials, and that gave them hope. This past June God brightened all our lives by blessing Steve and Keri with a big, healthy baby girl, Sierra Taylor!

Hardships will come! They will come in different shapes and sizes, some more obvious than others. Many will be difficult to understand. Even so, the widow of Nain allowed Jesus to move into her life and give life to her son. God's timing is different from ours— we wanted our babies for this life—God knew that only through these hardships would we have six children for eternity! God's answer for us will always be to trust him with all our heart, to walk by faith and to believe his promises. Then we, like the widow of Nain, will experience true, abundant life.

Gloria Baird
Los Angeles, USA

FOCUS   Which way will your hardships take you: away from God, giving Satan the victory, or closer to God, resulting in growth and promised blessings? What will help you make the right choice?

application questions on page 176

9

MARY OF BETHANY
Choose This Day

Mark 14:3-9; Luke 10:38-42; John 11:1-45; 12:1-8

Jerusalem was the hub of the Jewish world. All males 13 years old and older were commanded to attend three feasts a year in this city of David.[1] Thousands of pilgrims streamed into the city, eyes filled with wonder as they beheld the temple with its accompanying rituals and splendor. All homes were freely opened to guests during this time, but the large number of pilgrims sometimes overflowed to the nearby town of Bethany—a "Sabbath day's journey" (less than a mile) from Jerusalem. Both Bethany and her sister city, Bethphage, were "specially celebrated for their hospitality to pilgrim-guests."[2] How appropriate that Bethany was the home of special friends to Jesus, the true King of Jerusalem.

◆

Have you ever invited 13 hungry men to dinner? It is enough to cause even the most hearty hostess to tremble. A challenging proposition—even with electric stoves, refrigerators and microwaves. But this is precisely what Mary and Martha of Bethany did as they invited Jesus and his disciples into their home. Extensive preparations were in order.

A Woman of Priorities

Instead of running around frantically to ensure that the evening was perfect, Mary chose to sit and listen to Jesus. Martha, on the other hand, was fretting over the last-minute details and fuming that Mary wasn't doing her share. Surely to Martha's surprise, Jesus applauded Mary's choice. Most of us would have to admit that we relate to Martha. We have all thought, *Why aren't these people helping me?* What was Mary thinking? Was she really being insensitive to her sister? What did Jesus see in Mary that moved him to commend her choice?

---

[1]Boys could begin to attend the temple at 11 or 12 years of age.
[2]Alfred Edersheim, *Sketches of Jewish Social Life* (Peabody, Massachusetts: Hendrickson, 1994) 80.

As a Jewish woman, Mary knew how important hospitality was, but she understood that honoring the guest is the *heart* of hospitality.

At some point during Jesus' ministry, Mary had decided to make Jesus *the* priority of her life. His teaching and friendship had filled a void in her that nothing else had ever filled. Certainly other things in her life were important, but she knew that ultimately he held the keys to life and to God himself. The more she listened and heard what Jesus said, the more she believed that he was a special prophet sent by God—maybe even the Messiah. And on this occasion in her own home, she was determined not to lose a chance to sit at his feet and listen. She may have even begun to understand that Jesus' life was in danger and that each visit might be his last.

Life is busy for women. Our days are filled with demands: marriage, children, work, a house to keep and meals to make. And now in the '90s, with two-career families and single mothers the norm rather than the exception, life sometimes feels like it is stuck on a fast-speed setting and getting faster. We have much to learn about priorities from this "30s" woman.

A Woman of Peace

Mary may have been the quieter of the two sisters when they first met Jesus, but she was undoubtedly filled with turmoil inwardly. Like many women, she might have been worried, anxious, insecure or fearful. Only those who are in touch with their need drop everything to sit at the feet of Jesus. He was sensitive to her needs; he encouraged her to listen to him and learn. The more Mary heard Jesus' teachings, the more her mind and thinking were changed, and as her friendship with him grew, the more her heart changed. She began to trust him as she had never trusted anyone before. Her worries subsided. She felt freer, remembering his promise, "If you hold to my teaching, you are really my disciples. Then you will know the truth, and the truth will set you free" (John 8:31-32). For the first time in her life, she experienced a peace that no one could take away.

No relationship, however, is complete without testing, and Mary's relationship with Jesus was tested by tragedy when her brother Lazarus died. She knew Jesus would have come if he could have. She knew he loved Lazarus like his own brother. And yet, her heart was filled with anguish because Jesus wasn't there when she had desperately needed him, when her brother's life hung in the balance.

She had no doubt Jesus could have healed Lazarus, if only he had come in time.

When Jesus finally did arrive, he asked for Mary who quickly came to greet him, once again falling at his feet. When he saw Mary weeping, he was deeply moved and openly wept with her. God in the flesh comforted this woman who had become his friend.

Next, he amazed the town by raising Lazarus from the dead. The Jews generally believed that after a person died, the spirit hovered close by for three days. In their way of thinking, if for any reason the spirit and body were to be reunited, it would have to take place during this span of time. Possibly, Jesus had waited four days to raise Lazarus to show more clearly the power of God.

This moment was a turning point in Mary's faith. Her relationship with Jesus shifted from viewing him as her teacher and a great Rabbi to understanding his true role as her Lord and God. Peace that passes understanding came to her because she was now certain that Jesus was God and that God was in control of her life.

A Woman of Passion

Can you imagine, after grieving the death of your brother for four days, once again holding him and kissing him and looking into the eyes you had lovingly closed after his last breath was expelled? Seeing Jesus bring her brother back from the dead engulfed Mary with an incredible gratitude—a gratitude that ignited a deep passion to love him, to follow him, to serve him. She wanted to express her overflowing thankfulness for the salvation of Lazarus' physical life and her own spiritual life. Every day she thought of ways to express her gratitude—whether by sharing about his teaching, Lazarus' coming out of the grave or her own transformation from a woman beset by insecurities to a powerful disciple of Jesus. Every day she waited for word of when her friend and Lord would return to Bethany.

When he did, as the guest of Simon the Pharisee, she wanted to express her gratitude. What could she do? What could she give? Martha was already giving of her talent once again as she coordinated and served the dinner. Mary decided to take the most valuable perfume she owned and anoint Jesus. It was a small gesture, she thought, to say *Thank you, I love you, I would do anything for you.* The fragrance quickly filled the room, a reminder of Mary's deep love for him.

Jesus was moved, commenting, "She did what she could" (Mark 14:8). She didn't allow an intimidating situation to keep her from doing something special for Jesus. Certainly the most important people of the village would have been at this gathering. Nonetheless, Mary chose to interrupt the meal to perform a humbling service which drew not only attention to herself, but criticism as well. Clearly, serving Jesus was more important to her than protecting herself from the stares and raised eyebrows of others.

Jesus is looking for the same from us. He wants us to do what we can for him every day until the end of our lives. Only passion for God will carry us through the long haul. Like Mary, our passion for God should motivate us to give our best.

With great appreciation and love evident in both his voice and his eyes, Jesus said that whenever the gospel was told that Mary's action would always be remembered. He knew that Mary was fulfilled and happy as she gave in unrestrained fashion to him. He wanted to give her his best—heaven itself.

What is our best? Do we give it to God, or does he get the cheap cologne of our lives?

Being Jesus' Friend

The opportunity to be close to Jesus is a privilege. I remember as a little girl whispering my prayers at night, "Now I lay me down to sleep, I pray the Lord my soul to keep. And if I die before I wake, I pray the Lord my soul to take."

As a sophomore at the University of Florida, I lay in my bed saying the same rote prayer to a being who seemed like "the Unknown God." No one had ever taught me how to be close to God.

Then during the first few days of track practice, a teammate invited me to church. The previous summer I had dutifully gone to church every Sunday but had never found God. I eagerly accepted her invitation.

When I think of that first service, I remember seeing Jesus so vividly in the singing, preaching and in the loving manner of the people. I never wanted to leave. I'm sure that was how Mary felt when she sat at Jesus' feet. Like Mary, from my first days as a disciple, I have always wanted to be close to God and to give the kingdom my best. That desire does not always meet with applause from family, friends and bosses.

However, Mary's willingness to put her friendship with Jesus first and to fight to worship him means more to me today than ever before. I am desperate to imitate her. Life gets tougher as I get older. Making Jesus the priority in my life, being at peace and keeping the passion for God burning brightly becomes increasingly challenging.

To know God and Jesus, I must slow down. It takes quiet times, stillness, listening, praying and meditating to know God. To "be still and know that I am God" (Psalm 46:10) seems against our nature as women. How many of us would be friends with Jesus if he walked among us today? Would we be too busy *doing good*?

At age 38, I had our third child, Jackson, who joined our 11-year-old Katherine and 7-year-old Jonathan. He was a complete surprise. My planned family and orderly life was suddenly turned upside down. Staying close to Jesus has been harder than ever since his birth. I have never been less like Mary in my life. The demands of a new baby, a family and a church began to crowd out my first priority—Jesus.

However, God's plan for my life has caused me to fall at Jesus' feet with gratitude. I am challenged and inspired by Jesus' words, "From everyone who had been given much, much will be demanded; and from the one who has been entrusted with much, much more will be asked" (Luke 12:48). I truly have never been more thankful in my life! I know that God is in control, and I am grateful he blessed us with this third child, allowing me to enjoy motherhood longer. Studying Mary's life has been a complete joy. If I learn the lessons she has to teach me, I will have inner peace that will result in a passion for this lost world.

Kim Sapp
Atlanta, USA

 FOCUS Are you eager to sit at Jesus' feet daily? Judging by your actions, would Jesus say you were his friend?

application questions on page 176

10

MARTHA
Open Home, Disciplined Heart

Luke 10:38-42; John 11:1-44; 12:1-2

Contrary to what we may think, a Jewish woman in the first century did have certain rights:

◆ She could retain title to property brought into her marriage, but she could not sell it without her husband's consent. Also, he could not sell it without her consent.
◆ She could appoint agents to transact business for her.
◆ She could act as an agent in selling goods for her husband.
◆ In certain situations she could receive a divorce.

Those with the most autonomy were either unmarried adult daughters, divorcees or widows whose deceased husbands had a male heir. Anything these women earned was theirs to keep since they were not under the legal authority of a man. In all probability, Martha of Bethany was a widow who had full control of her assets.

Martha played a role of hospitality and support to Jesus and the disciples that subsequent women would play in the spread of the early church: Mary of Jerusalem, Lydia, Priscilla, Phoebe and Nympha. God used these women powerfully as they gave of their means to herald the good news that Jesus is Lord!

◆

The Teacher was on his way to their village. Martha had come to admire Jesus from the stories that she had heard about him and knew that he spoke with authority. She believed he could have a great impact on her, her family and her village. From everything she had heard, he was insightful, full of compassion, fair and just. She knew he respected women and allowed them to speak and interact with him, unlike most men of the time.

Being a woman of social standing, her opinions mattered to those around her. She was a woman with drive—orderly and efficient. She was respected and admired for her ability to reach out and meet the needs of others. Martha's hospitality was indicative of her passionate love for others. She was hardworking, very outspoken and sincere. The towns-people looked to Martha for input on social, family and business affairs. It was no surprise to the people that Jesus would recline at Martha's home.

A Close Friend

Jesus, like all of us, needed good friends. He needed people he felt comfortable with—people in whose homes he felt like family. Martha initiated and sustained such a relationship with this itinerant teacher, this Son of the Living God. She was bold and confident as she approached her friend. She had the gall to complain to Jesus that Mary was not helping her with preparations for their meal. His honest, direct and loving rebuke did not deter her or destroy their relationship (Luke 10:41-42). We can know they remained friends because it was apparently after this encounter that she went to Jesus concerning the death of Lazarus and even later that she served at a dinner honoring him. She did not withdraw or emotionally cut herself off from Jesus because he corrected her. Because of her assertive personality type, we might guess that this one recorded incident was not the only time Jesus had to bring her back to a spiritual perspective.

Jesus and Martha entered into a meaningful discipling relation-ship because Martha became his student, his servant and his devoted friend. She humbled herself with Jesus and allowed herself to be vulnerable—not the natural response of someone who tends to trust in her own strength of character. As a result, Martha must have learned to love Jesus as she had never loved anyone before.

The Bottom-Line Type

Martha was the kind of woman who wanted to make a difference. She was not content to sit back and watch as things happened; she stepped out and *made* things happen. On the one hand, she was organized, skilled and detail-oriented. On the other hand, she could be pushy, patronizing and disrespectful.

Not many people would have been able to help Martha the way Jesus did. He was tolerant, patient and kind toward her. He had vision for her life, honoring her strengths and discipling her weak-nesses. They became a part of the same team—a team determined to change the world.

We get a window into Martha's character as she approached Jesus after the death of Lazarus. "Lord, if you had been here, my brother would not have died" (John 11:21). She was clearly disappointed that Jesus had not come earlier because she knew that he could have kept her brother from dying. She may have perceived his delay in responding as a lack of effort and concern. It seems that her tone in talking with him is factual and intellectual, although we know she was hurting in her grief. Jesus responds to her gently and kindly, but factually and philosophically.

Compare Mary's approach. She made the same statement, "If you had been here, my brother would not have died" (John 11:32). But as she spoke, she fell at his feet and wept. Jesus' response was to weep with her. No talk about the resurrection. Her hurt went straight to his heart because she allowed him to share in it with her. "He was deeply moved in spirit and troubled" and simply asked, "Where have you laid him?" (John 11:33-34).

It seems quite possible that Martha went *at* Jesus with her question, whereas Mary went *to* Jesus. The one: a bottom-line, logical, sequential *thinker*. The other: a more emotional, heart-oriented *feeler*. But both were grieving; both were loved by Jesus; both had faith, and both were rewarded for their faith. Other than Peter, Martha is the only person recorded as saying specifically, "You are the Christ, the Son of God" (John 11:27). In spite of her weaknesses, Martha had a relationship with Jesus that was inspiring and worthy of imitation.

Jesus: Guest or Lord?

It has been an honor for me to have spent the last 13 years building a respectful, powerful relationship with Jesus. I am thankful for Martha because, as I think back over the years, she simply reminds me of me.

Before I became a Christian, I was a young woman wanting to make a difference in the world, but I was without direction. Through the years, I have had to learn some of the same lessons as Martha. I have had to learn not to take offense at leaders in my life, but to see these relationships as opportunities for me to grow spiritually. I have had to learn to trust and to believe the best about those who were leading me. I now believe that honoring others is better than being honored. I have grown in my trust so that I can be vulnerable and open about my weaknesses. Martha's weakness became her strength, as one who was goal-oriented went after a *relationship* with Jesus. I, too, am so thankful to be true friends with the leaders in my life.

I was cut to the heart by studying Martha's natural character, which must have been so offensive to Jesus. In some situations, she did not show the respect that was due a king, a Lord, the Son of God. I'm sure she did not submit to him because she did not recognize his authority in her life. During those times, Jesus was simply a guest in her home and not Lord. I have to be careful also. Jesus can become a guest again if my character weaknesses go unchecked. To continue to be humble requires continual discipling.

I was inspired by Martha's strength to persevere in her relationship with Jesus as he discipled her heart. She was strengthened by the challenges and did not allow herself to pull back. Unlike Martha, I have often allowed myself to pull back, to be hurt and discouraged when my character is challenged. I have allowed my faith to be shaken. Today I see that the only way to make a difference is to stay humble and serve God's people just as Martha did.

Just as God used Martha, he has used my life to impact other women. I have sat at the feet of, dined with and shaken the hands of some of the most respected leaders in the world. But, like Martha, I have come to the conclusion that there is nothing more honorable than serving those in God's family.

Emma Causey
Seattle, USA

 As a servant in God's kingdom, have you kept Jesus as the Lord of your life, or has he become a guest?

application questions on page 177

11

SAMARITAN WOMAN
Thirst for Righteousness

John 4:1-42

The cruel and godless Assyrians destroyed the Northern Kingdom of Israel around 725 B.C. Leaving only the agricultural workers, they deported the influential Israelites and repopulated their promised land with foreigners. More from superstition than from faith, these new Gentile residents brought in a Levitical priest to teach them "what the God of the land requires" (2 Kings 17:27). Thus, the Samaritans adopted a form of worship to the God of Abraham. This, coupled with the intermarriage of the Jews who were left in the land, was odious to the Jews. They felt complete contempt for these unworthy, presumptuous Gentiles and the half-breeds they begot. It ran far deeper than simple racial prejudice—deep enough to cause Jews of Jesus' day to refuse to pass through Samaria even if it meant a long, inconvenient detour. But Jesus was never affected by bigotry or religious superiority. Jesus was affected only by people—he loved them with all his heart.

◆

It started out like every other day before it. The cleaning, the cooking, the mending, and then, the daily trip to the well to draw water. It was quite a walk and she dreaded it. By mid-morning she was already tired. *If only it were a little closer to town! Oh well, at least it gives me a break from the drudgery of housework.*

Alone

Choosing to make the trip alone later in the morning, she avoided the pain caused by the stares and whispers of the town's women. She thought as she walked along that she really did dislike her life. Actually, she hated the monotony of it. It was all too predictable, and she hadn't had much success with men, either. Men, yes, even the plurality of the word made her nauseous. How many times as a little girl had she dreamed of one day marrying the man she would love and then living happily ever after? Isn't that every little girl's dream?

But as a child she didn't think about marriage problems, adultery or death. Those sweet childhood dreams had turned into a difficult reality. She felt so empty. So alone. She had to plan ahead. This man she was with would eventually die, or worse, leave her for another. The thoughts flooded into her mind: *What would I do if that happened? How would I survive? Where would I live? Should I marry him? Do I really love him? And why on earth am I thinking about it now? Hadn't I decided to take life one day at a time? I must. Certainly I have learned that I cannot rely on anyone, and least of all, a man. And most of the time I don't need anyone anyway, or do I?*

She saw a man sitting beside the well and braced herself for how he might look at her or what he might say to her. Trying to ignore him, she went about her business. *I'll just get my water and be on my way. I certainly don't need to have any more gossip about my personal life going around town. I can just hear it now, "She went to the well and met a man!"*

Accepted

"When a Samaritan woman came to draw water, Jesus said to her, 'Will you give me a drink?'" (John 4:7). She just looked at him. For a moment she was speechless. Jews normally wouldn't even pass through Samaria. Yet, here was a Jewish man speaking with her, a Samaritan woman, asking for a favor. Her curiosity got the better of her. Besides, there was something different about this man, something in his eyes. She felt a little uncomfortable without really knowing why, and challenged him with a question, "How can you ask me for a drink?" (John 4:9).

She looked into his eyes, but Jesus looked into her heart. He knew she wanted her life to be different. Jesus, desiring to meet her spiritual need, steered the conversation to a personal level, but she resisted by turning the focus back on him. She wasn't comfortable talking about herself. Too many people knew too much already, and she didn't want to be challenged or have to defend herself yet again. Besides, it had been too long since she had looked deep into her heart. Any time she found herself thinking more deeply, she would stop herself. It was too painful. And anyway, she wanted to know more about this man. She wanted him to talk about himself—tell who he was, where he came from—but he didn't.

Jesus knew her soul was thirsty (Matthew 5:6), and the most important thing to him at that moment was her spiritual condition. She didn't quite understand, but she was beginning to catch on. She was realizing that this man was different, that he had something to offer her that she desperately needed. Her spirits began to lift.

Aware

Jesus knew what was troubling this Samaritan woman. He knew what she had been thinking as she walked to the well. He knew her innermost heartaches, just as he knows ours (Romans 8:26-27). And he knew that, engrossed as she was in her daily problems, she had neglected the needs of her soul. "He told her, 'Go, call your husband and come back'" (John 4:16). *How does he know? Was he just guessing? Do those piercing eyes really see straight into my soul as they seem to?*

"'I have no husband,' she replied" (John 4:17). Jesus told her she was right in what she had said and continued to convict her about her life: "The fact is, you have had five husbands, and the man you now have is not your husband" (John 4:18). She changed the subject. Here we see the character of the Samaritan woman. When Jesus talked about living water, she talked about her physical needs. When Jesus spoke about her physical life, she began to talk about religion. (What did the place of worship have to do with whether or not she had a husband?)

This woman, like many of us, had mastered the art of spending endless hours in discussions, making long arguments in which she could completely hide her true feelings. She had lived the majority of her life this way. But deep in her heart were the stored-up stories of a coming hope for everyone—even for the Samaritans. He would be the Messiah, and he would make everything clear. For a moment those childhood dreams crept back into her sad, yet hopeful, heart.

Alive

Jesus Christ, the Son of God, the Savior of the world, had revealed himself to this nameless Samaritan woman. She knew that she must reveal to her people that the Messiah had finally come. All the way back into town she ran with the news. Her heart pounded with hope and purpose. *It seems too good to be true, but I know he must be the promised Messiah. I am truly happy for the first time since I can remember.* She had known from the moment she met him that he was different, yet she had not begun to imagine what lay in store for her or her people. She could never have imagined that she would be the vessel God would use to reach them. For her, Jesus bypassed Jewish rules and prejudices, and for him, she overcame her poor self-image and lack of confidence. How thankful she now felt for that long, dusty, wonderful walk to the well!

Closer Than You Think!

I must admit, when I first began studying the Samaritan woman, I wasn't sure if I would relate to her. She had been with at least six different men, whereas I've been married to my childhood sweetheart for 19 years. Also, as soon as she heard about Jesus, she converted almost her entire town! I have seen timidity in my own sharing of his message. However, as I looked more closely, I saw some very clear similarities. I was amazed.

Had I lived in the days of the Samaritan woman, I too would have gone to the well at a different time of day to avoid the gossipy women. It's called *conflict avoiding*. Instead of making the effort to change their opinion of me or my circumstances, I would simply have avoided them. Even as I write this I think, *How nauseating!* Conflict avoiding is not listed in the Bible as a sin, but it is covered in the following: selfishness, lack of love, cowardice, not doing the good we need to and "the like" (Galatians 5:21). I know that when I am guilty of that sin, I am miserable until I do the right thing and deal with whatever the situation is—whether it's with a sister, a non-Christian friend or myself. I know I've grown and changed in this area, but it still lurks there in the dark, waiting to grab me when I am weak (Genesis 4:7).

I also related to the Samaritan woman in her hesitation to talk about herself. Growing up, I knew the doctrine of my church *to the letter*. You could have asked me just about anything, and I would have known the correct teaching of the church on that subject. But I never wanted to get on a personal level (not that anyone ever asked me anything personal). I wasn't even real with *myself*, much less anyone else. I have most definitely learned that the only way to get help and be a true disciple is to share your heart with others. Don't let Satan deceive you. You never get too old, too mature or too smart to need other people in your life.

Just recently, I was feeling frustrated about my personal life and ministry. It helped so much to talk with and get advice from trusted leaders and friends. I know so many women who don't want to be open because they have felt betrayed or have been hurt before. Have I been hurt? Has a trust been broken by someone to whom I opened up at some point? Sure, but I have been helped and loved many, many more times, and the blessings far outweigh anything "bad" I may have experienced. I have had to realize that no one except God is perfect. People will make mistakes. I will make mistakes. But God says we need each other and he gives us grace to grow and forgive. So there really is no excuse for not sharing our hearts, is there?

And finally, the level of gratitude displayed by the Samaritan woman is challenging to me. A spirit of gratitude is something I pray for just about every day. I am grateful for Jesus and his sacrifice, my husband and children, and special friends who are disciples. Realizing these blessings keeps me faithful. And, of course, the natural response to gratitude is to share what you have with others.

Tears came to my eyes as I was closing out my chapter and reread her words, "Come, see a man who told me everything I ever did. Could this be the Christ?" At that moment I felt her pain lift and her hope return. Yes, she was a real woman. Yes, she did exist. Yes, we can and must learn from her, for don't we all long to hear these same words as we share with others, "We no longer believe just because of what you said; now we have heard for ourselves, and we know that this man really is the Savior of the world"?

Donna Lamb
Miami, USA

 Do you try to change the focus of a conversation when it gets too close to your heart? Or are you willing to be open and vulnerable?

application questions on page 177

12

JOANNA
A Gutsy Follower

Luke 8:1-3; 23:49, 55-56; 24:1-12

A carpenter's son from Nazareth was roaming the countryside on foot, attracting crowds wherever he went. His teachings were compelling, insightful and authoritative. He often taught in parables and quoted knowledgeably from the Scriptures. He never backed off from a challenging question and never lost a debate. And if there was any chance that he might be dismissed as just another philosopher, he performed miracle after miracle to confirm that his message had a divine source.

Gravity was defied, winds were calmed, and waves were stilled. The lame were healed, the blind were given sight, lepers were cleansed, the dead were raised, and demons lost their battles before a superior power. Some of those healed he allowed to accompany him; others he sent back to their homes. Some he encouraged to share their stories, others he charged to tell no one. His fame spread widely. Even those who had never met him had opinions about him because of the things they had heard.

Herod the tetrarch himself was curious and hoped to meet him someday. That meeting would finally occur on the day Pilate sent Jesus to be tried before Herod. But two or three years prior to that trial, could it be that Herod's curiosity was first peaked by the wife of one of his own servants?

◆

She is only mentioned twice and only in the book of Luke. Someone once observed that the Holy Spirit does not waste ink. There are important lessons to be learned from Joanna. Otherwise God would not have included her name in the story of his Son.

When we first meet Joanna in Luke 8, we find her in a very elite group. She numbered among a few women who accompanied Jesus and the Twelve, traveling with them from town to town. She had been profoundly affected by him, having been healed of either a physical malady or demon-possession. She had heard the parables and witnessed the miracles.

She was married. Her husband, Cuza, was employed by Herod Antipas, tetrarch of Galilee, but often referred to as "king"—one of the more prominent and powerful enemies of the man she loved and followed (Luke 13:31). She had some money of her own, and she gave it to Jesus for his ministry and support. Her loyalty to a controversial troublemaker was probably awkward for her husband. His boss's father had tried to kill the child Jesus (Matthew 2:13-20), and now it was Herod's kingship that was threatened by this new "King of the Jews."

Many pressures could have worn her down and caused her to give up on the initial exuberant gratitude that made her risk so much to follow Jesus. But she stuck with him until the very end. She was in the crowd that heard the parable of the sower (Luke 8:4-15), and perhaps when Jesus talked about the seed springing up quickly with joy, she thought of her own conversion. When he warned of falling away because of a lack of roots, perhaps it produced in her a conviction to make her roots go deep enough to withstand the tests that life would surely bring.

The Test of Perseverance

It is hard to imagine, considering her husband's career, that he would be very supportive of his wife's faith, especially considering her visibility, the time commitment and the financial implications. I can hear his tirades: "You are making me look like a fool. You are a threat to my job. I thought you believed in submission." It is speculation, of course, but I suspect she faced opposition from many sources.

I often think of seeing her in heaven someday. I have so many questions to ask to fill in the gaps from Luke 8 to Luke 24. In the latter, she is mentioned as "Joanna," not "Joanna, the wife of Cuza." Maybe it doesn't mean anything at all. Or maybe it does. Maybe he died. And then, maybe he divorced her when he forced her to choose between himself and Jesus, and she chose Jesus. Maybe Herod pressured Cuza. At any rate, I wish Luke 24 could read, "Joanna and Cuza, former manager of Herod's household, returned from the empty tomb..."

Whatever the events of those intense years, she persevered through the bright times and the dark times, hanging on to a commitment that saw her through to the very end. I long for the time when I can sit at her feet and hear her story and tell her how much I admired her even from the little I knew.

The Test of Heartbreak

She was, no doubt, among "the women who followed him from Galilee, [who] stood at a distance, watching [the crucifixion]" (Luke 23:49). She must have followed Joseph of Arimathea after he claimed the battered body and took it to the tomb (Luke 23:55). She was probably up all night with the other women preparing the spices and perfumes as a final tender service to the man they had adored. It was certainly a unique girl's night out—subdued conversation, busy hands, questions, memories, tears, smiles, shattered dreams, uncertain hope. It must have been an uneasy rest that Sabbath while they waited to visit the tomb on Sunday.

The Test of Danger

She surely understood the danger of displaying her loyalty to this rebel at his execution. The men definitely understood. Peter denied Jesus three times, while the rest deserted him and went into hiding. They did not risk visiting the tomb until the guards were gone—since no corpse was left to guard. Perhaps it was an advantage being a woman. Perhaps they were considered no serious threat in that culture; insignificant and sentimental, they were free to go through their little rituals of grief and be done with it.

Nevertheless, I am inspired by Joanna and the other women who risked the danger of association with an executed criminal. Their love and gratitude produced a faith and courage that enabled them to be loyal against all odds.

The Test of Disrespect

Sometimes the people who ought to offer the greatest encouragement and support will disappoint you.

> ...Joanna and the others...told this [the empty tomb report] to the apostles. But they did not believe the women because their words seemed to them like nonsense (Luke 24:10-11).

What an insult! Of all the people who should have believed them, the apostles topped the list. But the other victories of her faith make me confident that she rose above her pride to avoid the temptation of a spiteful, critical nature that might have said, "How dare these self-righteous cowards dismiss us so glibly. We are eyewitnesses and we know we are right!" She remembered, I am sure, Jesus words: "Forgive and you will be forgiven...Why do you look at the speck in your brother's eye and pay no attention to the plank in your own eye?" (Luke 6:37-42). She doesn't seem like a woman who would pass every other test and then give in to pettiness.

Joanna, a loyal friend and follower of Jesus. He turned her life and her world upside down, and she refused to allow anyone to turn it back.

Enduring Gratitude

I am challenged most by the gratitude in Joanna's life that produced her perseverance. She was saved from not only a specific ailment, but more importantly, from spiritual death. My gratitude for what I have been saved from should motivate a faith, love and courage great enough to make me persevere through any test. I never want to forget what I would be like without Jesus, and I want that to be the motivating force in my life to the very end.

I used to read Titus 2:3 ("Likewise, teach the older women to be reverent in the way they live, not to be slanderers or addicted to much wine, but to teach what is good.") and wonder why older women would be vulnerable to an addiction to wine. Living now in my fifth decade, I have a hunch that addiction to wine was the retirement mentality of the first century: a little relaxation, a little escape from responsibility, a little edge off the aches and pains.

My zeal is no longer fed by youthful energy. The zeal for living a reverent, productive life has to come from a deeper source of conviction, gratitude and love that must be renewed daily. I realized recently that I had grown tired and dull. A combination of circumstances, including recurring fatigue (a symptom of my rheumatoid arthritis) had tested me, and I had failed the test. I pushed through the routines of my days attending to the most visible demands. I did not think through my priorities and the efficient use of the energy I did have. I did not apply my creativity to make things work. Everything had grown dull—my quiet times, my discipline, my evangelism.

A single lesson at a midweek service became my wake-up call from God. It was hard getting focused again to prioritize my days and delegate the tasks better done by someone else. It was harder still to eliminate some activities that were nonproductive. Those hard changes probably would have been impossible to make without the helpful input of objective discipling. I desperately needed someone else's spiritual perspective.

Repentance is sweet, and I saw God's blessings immediately, including a sense of increased energy as I felt more fulfillment from being more productive. James 1:3 says that perseverance is produced by the testing of your faith. In addition, it is motivated by gratitude and love and is encouraged by discipline.

Linda Brumley
Seattle, USA

 How high is your gratitude level? Does it motivate you to persevere?

application questions on page 178

13

WIDOW AT THE TEMPLE
Out of Her Poverty

Mark 12:35-44; Luke 21:1-4

The compassionate heart of God is never seen more clearly than in the Mosaic injunctions to care for widows. When a woman lost her husband to death, she not only lost the comfort and security of his companionship, but his financial support as well. If she still had children at home, her burden was increased. She had no insurance policies, no Social Security, no welfare. What she did have, though, was a loving God who instructed his people to meet her needs:

> At the end of every three years, bring all the tithes of that year's produce and store it in your towns, so that the Levites (who have no allotment or inheritance of their own) and the aliens, the fatherless and the widows who live in your towns may come and eat and be satisfied, and that the Lord your God may bless you in all the work of your hands (Deuteronomy 10:18).

During the time of Jesus, special collections were taken to supply food to the widows. But, even with this help, these vulnerable women were often desolate and impoverished—easy prey for exploitation.

◆

The city was alive with activity. The marketplace was teeming with excitement. The streets were filled with people—businessmen, housewives, servant girls, religious leaders—all bustling about. And moving through the crowd was a poor widow, making her way toward the temple. As her eyes caught a glimpse of the temple, her steps quickened. The woman eagerly hurried on her way, clutching a small bag in her hand.

Eager to Give
Approaching the temple, she noticed a large crowd. Someone was teaching, so the woman pressed her way through the curious bystanders.

The teacher was talking about loving God with all your heart, soul, mind and strength. Somehow, the tone of his teaching seemed different from the Pharisees' teaching. She always felt condemned and shut out when they talked. But with this man she felt warmed and welcomed. And he spoke with such authority. He had not quoted one rabbi since she had entered the temple court. He went on to warn the people about doing things for show and using widows for personal gain. When the man finished teaching, he sat down. Talking with his disciples, he glanced at the people as they brought their offerings to the collection box.

The poor widow was even more joyful and excited now. She did love God, and she did feel so loved by God. She took the tiny bag she held in her hand and emptied its contents into the box—two very small copper coins. The woman did not seem to notice the wealthy people ahead of her, throwing in large amounts. She did not appear to be embarrassed or ashamed by her meager offering. One thought alone filled her heart: God has given me everything. I must give him all that I have. She placed the two small coins in the temple treasury and walked away happy and thankful.

Giving Up Everything

Can't you just imagine this humble woman, excitedly anticipating giving her gift to God? We do not know for certain what she was thinking that day, but we can know her motives were pure because Jesus knew what was in her heart as he affirmed her actions. Had she had some ulterior motive, he would have known it and would not have offered her as an example of wholehearted giving. A poor woman, a widow with no real source of income and only two small coins left—and she gave it ALL! What a heart!

What did giving up everything mean for this woman? First, it meant she had given up control. There was nothing left to hold on to. What little control she had over her sparse finances was given over totally to God. She was completely dependent and vulnerable. It would have been very easy for her to be anxious or self-pitying, but she did not excuse herself from "giving everything" because of her circumstances. The widow could have thought, *I have nothing to give, but I'll go to receive my widow's allotment.* Instead, she came to give, eagerly and gladly. She had learned the lesson taught by the man who watched her in the temple that day: "It is more blessed to give than to receive" (Acts 20:35). She did not selfishly or desperately hold on to what she had because she trusted God to take care of her (2 Corinthians 9:8).

It was surely difficult for this woman to be in such a vulnerable, dependent position, but this is where we must all start. *Giving everything* will head us down the path to humility because it means we have put our trust in God. Too often we put our trust in material goods or relationships. We think there is security in fleeting things. Unlike the widow, we hold on to things that we will lose someday anyway. Our giving is in proportion to our faith and trust in God.

This radical woman gave every cent she had. She gave beyond what she could see. She put herself out on the edge. What would she eat? How would she live? Those thoughts may have never entered her mind. How could she give all that she had? This woman gave it all because she knew she had been given everything. She was so grateful. She remembered how needy she had been and how much she had been given. As a result, she wanted to give her best.

Surely she had heard of the widow of Zarephath (1 Kings 17:7-24). Jesus refers to God's graciousness to her as she gave to his prophet, Elijah (Luke 4:24-26). She had only enough flour and oil to make one last meal for her son and herself. But, by faith, she made bread and brought it to the Lord's prophet as he had requested. The result? The promise was given by God: "The jar of flour will not be used up and the jug of oil will not run dry until the day the Lord gives rain on the land" (1 Kings 17:14). God was true to his promise, as always. For the remaining three years of the famine, her needs were met miraculously. The spirit of this trusting widow was alive at the temple that day as her first-century counterpart dropped her coins into the box. The Spirit of the God who never changes was also alive at the temple that day, ready to bless her giving heart.

Thoughtless or Thoughtful?

Jesus is very aware of what we give. He wants to see where our hearts are. On this occasion he sat down purposefully to watch the people as they gave. He noticed that the wealthy people thoughtlessly tossed in their contributions. Maybe for them it was not such a great privilege and honor to give. Maybe they had not thought about to whom the gift was going. Or, perhaps, there was no sacrifice in their giving because they had not thought of giving their best. It was just a habit to give, or it was just the right thing to do, but in either case, these thoughtless givers did not have hearts motivated by love and gratitude, focused on giving to God.

Yet, this poor widow was a thoughtful giver. Just as anyone would plan and save and anticipate giving a gift to someone she loves, this woman was bringing a gift to the love of her life. She might have even felt disappointed that she did not have more to give. Even though she had very little, she did not hold back anything for herself. Why? It is only natural to sacrifice for those we love. It comes from the overflow of the heart. Our "first love" gets first priority. When there is no sacrifice involved, giving is a thoughtless and loveless gesture.

Jesus was so impressed by the widow's gift that he called his disciples over to tell them what he had just seen. He who was giving his all, had witnessed the outpouring of a grateful, faithful and loving heart. Her heart mirrored his own. We need to be challenged by those who give everything, and we should change to become like them.

We must examine our own hearts, knowing that Jesus watches as we give—just as he did at the temple that day. *How thoughtful is my giving? What sacrifices do I make with my time, emotions, money, desires or relationships? Would Jesus use my giving as an example to others? Does my heart mirror the heart of God as the heart of this first-century widow did?* Is it time to clean the mirror?

Holding On or Giving Up

Should I give up or should I hold on? A heart-level tug of war. How many times have I played this childish game? I start out excited and determined to give, but then somewhere along the line, I turn the focus in on *me*, and then I hang the "CLOSED" sign out, and there is no more giving.

Five years ago we sold everything, packed up the troops and headed to Abidjan, Ivory Coast. Selling our possessions did not seem like such a hard thing to do at the time. In fact, it was sort of liberating. It was only later, after we settled into our new place, that reality hit. I felt the loss—and not just with the material things. I had given up my closest friends, my family, my culture, my language—everything that was familiar and natural. I had thoughts that maybe it was a foolish decision to make such a radical move. I had nothing left. But that is exactly where God wanted me—realizing that everything comes from him and that I have nothing without him. I had to learn to be vulnerable, give up the control, and depend totally on God. What a blessing that lesson has been. God simply humbled me.

Yet the learning is not over. During this past month, God has exposed my heart again. I have seen my resistance to "giving it all," especially in my marriage. I was very aware of Mark's needs, yet I would politely bow out of giving because of being "tired" or "emotionally drained." Put more honestly, I was just being selfish. I have seen that it is much easier for me to work hard physically and meet needs in that way, but in the process everyone around me comes out on the short end of the stick emotionally. I have wanted to set the limits and maintain the control of how much I give—and on what level I give. With my children, I have seen that I will give to a certain point as well. It is in the emotional arena again that I tend to hold back.

I have had to learn how to keep giving my heart and to persevere and to keep believing the best through difficult situations. Instead of focusing on the obstacles, I am learning to be faithful and positive and to believe in change—no matter how long it takes. When I give the control to God, my heart is free to give everything. And, you know, it is a funny thing how God always makes things come out all right.

So whether it is where I live, how I live, or with whom I live, I must have a heart that wants to give everything—a grateful, humble, trusting heart just like the poor widow. She has amazed me, humbled me, inspired me and changed me, and yet, I know there will be even more to come. Thank God that he keeps changing me as I keep giving to him.

Diane Ottenweller
Johannesburg, South Africa

 Think of what you have given in the last month. When have you struggled to give everything ? When has your giving been thoughtful?

application questions on page 178

14
MOTHER OF THE BLIND MAN
I Will Not Fear

John 9:1-41

Synagoge—transliterated *synagogue*—means "a bringing together." These special places of Jewish worship sprang up in the *diaspora*, Jewish communities outside Palestine, originating during the Babylonian exile. Cut off from the temple and sacrifices, they pulled together to worship and read the law, to maintain their heritage and sense of community. By the time of Jesus, most cities had many synagogues; Jewish legend claimed the existence of more than 400 in Jerusalem itself. A quorum of 10 Jewish men made possible the establishment of a synagogue. In the larger cities, those of like nationality or trade pulled together and started their own synagogue—their *belonging place*. Being "put out" of the synagogue would have devastated a Jew both spiritually and socially. Any indication that someone believed in the deity of Jesus of Nazareth would have meant sure expulsion.

◆

Blind? Are you sure? Blind? Why that means...no, it can't be! The rumors would begin spreading rapidly through the neighborhood and village. A son, born blind. The questions filled her mind. After waiting for years, hadn't she felt blessed by God to be able to finally bear a child? *Where is God now? I had longed for this birth. All the months of feeling this tiny presence deep inside me. The dreams and hopes—and now this. It will surely be seen as a curse. Blind people almost always become beggars for lack of any other chance of employment. It must be a punishment from God. The rabbis have so often taught that terrible punishment comes upon children because of the sin of their parents. But for which sin? Haven't I held to the teachings? What have I done that was so awful?*

Why, God?

The years wore on. As she looked at her son struggling and stumbling along, she felt such love for him, and yet felt such shame. The people whispered about her son, the beggar, as she went by. She sensed their scorn and disdain for whatever sin had caused such a disgrace. Her fear that he wouldn't be accepted by others as "normal" was realized.

One Sabbath she listened as the rabbi read a prophecy from Isaiah about the promises of God, "Then will the eyes of the blind be opened and the ears of the deaf unstopped" (Isaiah 35:5). She had wondered about this strange promise. *What could it mean? Why would God promise this and yet allow my son to be blind? Where is God? Didn't he promise to bless his people?* She was disappointed with life. She felt a right to feel sorry for herself.

What Now?

When we meet this devastated mother, her son has been healed. We would expect to find her weeping with joy and thankfulness, to be searching for the one who had made a dream come true. But instead we find her tight-lipped and anxious as she and her husband cautiously approach the Pharisees. They always had been the final authority in all matters; therefore the acceptance or rejection of these religious leaders would impact the rest of her life. The Pharisees were so angry about this "Jesus" and had said that anyone who acknowledged him to be the Messiah would be cast out of the synagogue. No doubt she had heard the claims of this man: that he *said* he was the Messiah and the light of the world. Had she heard of the miracles he had performed? Had she secretly hoped he might really be who he said he was?

Why Me?

What a mystifying day it had been. Early that morning, all the neighbors ran through the streets yelling that some blind person could now see. Of course she had rushed to the door to see what was happening, and there he stood—her son. Whole. Seeing. And for the first time in his life, he saw his mother and looked into her eyes. He could barely speak because of his excitement. She was so filled with amazement that she could only stammer out the questions, *"How?" "Who?"*

But the joy of the moment faded quickly as the officials sent word that she and her husband should report to them immediately. Fear loomed in her heart. *What do they want with me? What do they think I've done?* She stood trembling before them, hearing their accusations against her son and the one who had healed him. What should she say? It was clear to her that anyone who would admit to such a miracle, and on the Sabbath, would be condemned by the Pharisees and thrown out of the synagogue. Somehow she got the answers out, "Yes, of course, he is our son. Yes, he was born blind. No, we don't know who opened his eyes. Why not ask him?" It all happened so quickly. In pushing the responsibility on her son, she felt she had ensured her place in the "synagogue-community." *Surely my son will understand my need to protect our standing in the synagogue.*

His mother did not see the working of God through this miracle. During a time when she should have stood by her son, she chose to protect herself. She experienced the paralyzing effect of fear. It took control and kept her from thinking and acting clearly. It blocked her from seeing what was really important, really eternal. On the other hand, her son, responding with joy and boldness, lifted up seeing eyes to the Son of God and worshiped him. That day, those who were blind could see, and those who could see became blind.

God Will Lead Us to Victory!

Spending time with this mother revealed to me that I can react as she did. The mother was concerned that God wasn't doing his part. She was fearful and anxious about her position and her future. She worried about what others thought. I can be like her if I don't remember that God is active in my life—no matter how things may look.

Worry is actually another name for fear—fear of what may or may not happen. In 1 Peter 3:6 (Phillips translation) we are called not to give way to "hysterical" fears. When I arrived in Germany several years ago with a 5-year-old and a 3-month-old, I was unable to speak the language and fearful about many things. One of my fears was that my youngest daughter would grow up speaking German as her heart language and not be able to communicate deeply with me. A dear friend looked straight at me, and said, "Janet, don't you have enough to worry about *today*?" Funny how something so simple can slip your mind. Her question reminded me how utterly foolish I am to fret about things that haven't even happened. My daughter, at 6-and-a-half, speaks fluent English and German, and we have a fantastic friendship!

What *do* we need to worry about? Our father in heaven knows what we need and has promised to take care of us, just as he had promised this fearful mother. We must decide to remember God's promises and keep putting our life in his hands. We must trust that he has the ability to work powerfully in any situation!

This is a lesson I must keep learning. The last few months have been a struggle for fruit in my life and in the church in Munich. I became frustrated and complained to God, "Why do you bless others and not me?" and "Which sin is it?" and "Am I so much worse than everyone else that you withhold blessings in my life?"

Basically, I was responding to a challenging situation much as the disciples did when they encountered the blind man. They asked, "Who sinned, this man or his parents, that he was born blind?" (John 9:2). In other words, *Who's to blame for this difficult situation?*

How ashamed I was to discover such selfishness and ingratitude! Hasn't God saved me and poured out his grace in my life? That alone is far more than I deserve. I must not forget that the blind man was healed, his sight restored and he turned to worship God! God has blessed me abundantly as well! I can and should be thankful to God in difficult times, especially when the situation seems insurmountable. It is *then* God will be magnified as he brings about a great victory! Whether the mother became a disciple of Jesus, we do not learn. I hope she got to meet Jesus. I hope she repented and confronted her fearful heart. But today we have to think about us. We have to confront the fears in our hearts by approaching difficulties with confidence, knowing full well that God is on our side (Proverbs 29:25). God will be glorified only if we don't give up or give way to fear!

Janet Marks
Providence, USA

 Do difficult situations cause you to doubt God's working in your life? List 10 ways God has blessed you. Thank and praise him for how he has worked in your life.

application questions on page 178

15

SYROPHOENICIAN WOMAN
Such Great Faith

Matthew 15:21-28; Mark 7:24-30

Tyre was a coastal city of Phoenicia, famous for ships, merchants and trading. Isaiah prophesied against the city, "Wail O ships of Tarshish! For Tyre is destroyed and left without house or harbor" (Isaiah 23:1). He referred to her as the "marketplace of the world" (23:3). She was a city that did not know or honor the one true God.

From this city came visitors to hear the Jewish teacher from Galilee—a three-day journey by foot. "A great number of people from the coast of Tyre and Sidon" came to hear the message that we would later call the Sermon on the Mount (Luke 6:17). "Do not give dogs what is sacred..." (Matthew 7:6), Jesus said in his sermon. This comment would take on a different meaning during a visit to Tyre later in his ministry.

◆

What in the world is he talking about?" thought the apostle. "Washing hands, honoring parents, eating food, clean and unclean...what did it all mean?" Peter wanted to ask Jesus to explain what he had just been talking about, but the last time he tried that Jesus called him "dull." He decided to be content with following his master to the vicinity of Tyre for a retreat and hoped that when Jesus fell asleep, he could discuss things with the other guys. Little did the apostle know that a pagan woman from Syrian Phoenicia was about to become a visual aid he would never forget.

"Your request is granted" (Matthew 15:28). How sweet those words must have sounded to this desperate woman. Jesus did an amazing miracle in her life—he healed her daughter. We all want Jesus to do miracles in our lives, but sometimes we doubt it can happen to us. This woman was not even a "God-fearing Greek," and Jesus did a miracle for her! However, Jesus did not just grant her request; he commended her for her faith. Not many people were praised for their faith by Jesus. In fact, the apostles were challenged again and again for their *lack* of faith. Why did Jesus affirm her faith?

Faith of a Mother

"*Enough!*" *Horaya screamed in her heart as she witnessed yet another outburst by her previously gentle and loving daughter. The woman cradled her 10-year-old in her arms, rocking and weeping at the same time.*

Her daughter had been acting noticeably different over the past year and recently had become out of control. Her mother-in-law recognized the signs...demon-possession. Horaya's local medium had told her to visit the temple of Asherat, "The Lady of Tyre and Goddess of Sidon."* Unfortunately, the high priestess at the temple had divined no answers when she had cut open the birds to look at their intestines. The pagan woman received nothing from her gods that day. She returned home and pounded the wall in despair.

Her cousin, who had been living in Galilee for a few years, heard about Horaya's daughter. He told her stories of a man named "Jesus" who could heal people and cast out demons. He was filled with the power of a god named "Jehovah." The woman had heard tales of "Baal," "El," "Anat," and "Asherat" since childhood but never of this "Jehovah."

Horaya met a man who said he was a servant for a Jewish leader named Jairus. This man claimed that Jesus had raised his master's daughter from the dead! According to him, the girl had been dead for an hour or so before Jesus arrived at their house, yet she was alive when he next saw her!

Afraid to get her hopes up, Horaya feared this was something that could never happen to her since she was not an Israelite. However, her persistent cousin told her that Jesus had a reputation for speaking with known sinners, women and even with non-Jews. He mentioned a Samaritan woman living near the Decapolis as an example.

That was all Horaya needed to hear. From that moment on, she was determined to see Jesus. No matter what it would take, she would find Jesus, and she would get her daughter healed! Nothing could stop her, for she was desperate and humble, and she believed.

Desperation

"As soon as she heard about him," "crying out," "fell at his feet," "begged." These phrases describe the Syrophoenician woman's first encounter with Jesus. We cannot help but be amazed at her determination. Even after being ignored by Jesus, seen as a pest by the apostles, rejected by Jesus and finally downright insulted, our pagan

---

*Theodor H. Gaster, *The Oldest Stories in the World* (Boston: Beacon Press, 1958) 194.

example did not give up. Her belief in Christ was not just wishful thinking...she did something! No wonder Jesus said she had great faith—the woman was desperate! But why? What could possibly motivate her to persevere like this? The answer is obvious—love! Because real love is desperate.

The Syrophoenician woman loved her daughter so much that she was desperate to get her out of Satan's grip. We have to be just as desperate to get people out of the kingdom of darkness. Our pagan friend teaches us to feel their pain and to love them enough to be desperate.

Bold Humility

The Syrophoenician woman is one of the best examples of humility in the Bible. She may have been a woman of standing among her own people—about that we will never know. What we do know is that she passed the test of humility as a pagan, where many Israelites, God's chosen people, had failed.

Matthew, who probably saw the encounter, recorded her humility beautifully. First, he revealed that she cried out to Jesus for mercy. That act alone is already humbling, but then Jesus refused to acknowledge her. When the apostles saw Jesus ignoring the woman, they told their master to "get rid of her." Instead of running away in shame, she stood her ground. Even when Jesus rebuffed her with the statement about not throwing the children's bread to dogs, she answered with cleverness, good humor, courage and patience.

Jesus loved her as much as he loved anyone. He simply had the mission to bring the message primarily to the Jews, knowing that it would spread to other people after his ascension. She graciously made allowances for what she must have taken to be his national and professional pride, and assuredly acknowledged the fact that Jesus could still bless her if he chose to do so. She could have become defensive and arrogant: *How dare you speak to me this way?* or *Who do those Jews think they are?* or *It's not fair...I always get the crumbs!* or *I thought you might be different from the others, but I was wrong.* She also could have become insecure and full of self-doubt: *It's true. I am a dog. I probably don't even deserve the crumbs. I'd better go home. Sorry for bothering you.* But instead of lecturing Jesus on not being rude or dissolving into tears and walking away, our woman remained firm in her expectation and asked for a miracle one more time. That is bold humility!

The Syrophoenician could not be arrogant with Jesus; she already knew that she did not even deserve to be in his presence, much less to ask him for a miracle. She could not get angry about the "crumbs"; when we know that we deserve nothing, we are grateful for anything. At the same time, she could not be insecure with Jesus because she was focused on her daughter's need and on God's power; therefore, worrying about self was out of the question. Because the Syrophoenician woman was conscious only of her need, and not of herself, she was able to take any challenge and show real humility before God. She had great faith, so she focused on God. She was truly humble, because real humility is not self-focused.

Regaining My First Love

Of all the things I saw in "my woman" over the past month, I was most convicted by her desperate love. I started out my Christian life wanting to save the world: door-knocking my dorm, street preaching in London, going off to start churches around Asia. Unfortunately, I have since fallen into the sin of not personally making disciples, under the guise of being busy with "important church matters."

At a recent conference, I was extremely challenged and inspired by the speeches to renew my love for the lost and to be personally fruitful again. I was cut to the heart! Three years had passed since I had met someone who became a Christian, and I call myself a leader!

I came back to South Asia and immediately began to share my faith. I prayed for God to soften my heart and give me the love for the lost that I had in the beginning of my walk with him. Still, not much was happening in the way of fruit.

While studying about the Syrophoenician woman, I was struck by her desperate attitude. I realized that was what I was missing. I needed a desperate love for people who are under Satan's control and need to be healed! Because of my conviction to have desperate love, I began sharing with people out of the overflow of my heart, even when I would have normally kept quiet because I was "in a hurry."

I began a "fruit fast" three times a week for a month. One friend began studying the Bible and two more agreed to get together soon. I even fell on my knees before a brother who had been struggling off and on for two years and begged him to repent! That is certainly not my natural character, but I remembered "my woman" and imitated her desperate love.

I'm so grateful for her example and the way she, through this Bible study, has changed my life. Others will become Christians soon because of my changes.

We can learn much from this pagan. She knew she was nothing, compared to God. She cried out to Jesus on behalf of someone she loved, someone in the grip of Satan. As we imitate her by being desperate for others' salvation and not focusing on ourselves, we, too, shall see people we love in the grip of Satan being set free. We, too, shall see Jesus doing miracles in our lives. And we, too, shall hear Jesus' words of praise, "Woman, you have great faith! Your request is granted."

Karen Louis
Sydney, Australia

 FOCUS

Are you as desperate to help people get out of Satan's grip now as you were when you first came into God's kingdom?

application questions on page 179

16
PILATE'S WIFE
Act on Truth

Matthew 27:11-26

Power politics and self-advancement motivated the Roman-appointed governors of captured nations. Pilate, governor of Judea, was no exception. The power of life and death was bequeathed to the governors by the Emperor himself. In an easily excitable province like Judea, that responsibility could be complicated by issues that were nonsensical to the religiously uninitiated—especially the situation introduced by a Galilean who claimed to be the Son of Israel's God. Jesus had no heritage, no prominent connections, no political influence. Why should Pilate care? Guilty or not guilty? How could Pilate know? The verdict: not guilty. The sentence: death by crucifixion. A spineless paradox that was true to form for a Roman governor of a detestable, difficult-to-rule province.

If one were writing a play portraying the week before the crucifixion, the role of Pilate's wife would be a bit part. In fact, she might never even appear on stage. In the biblical account, we see her husband receive a one-sentence message from her. That's all. And yet, the Spirit, through Matthew, recorded her comment for all time: "Don't have anything to do with that innocent man, for I have suffered a great deal today in a dream because of him" (Matthew 27:19).

Afflicting the Comfortable

Tradition tells us that her name was Claudia Procula and that she was the granddaughter of the Roman Emperor Augustus. Though tradition also tells us that she was possibly a Jewish convert or even a follower of Jesus,[1] all we know for sure is that she was the pampered wife of the highest official in Judea. Most of her hours were spent at the governor's residence at Caesarea, located on the shores of the Mediterranean Sea. When we first hear of her, she had traveled 40

---

[1] Edith Deen. *All of the Women of the Bible.* (New York: Harper and Roe Publishers, 1955) 206-207.

miles inland to Jerusalem with her husband and entourage, and was staying in the resplendent palace of Herod the Great. We can imagine the luxury of her bedroom chamber as she slept fitfully during the early morning hours on the day Jesus was to appear before her husband for judgment. Since the Jewish leaders were not allowed to execute anyone, they had to come to Pilate to do their dirty work.

We do not know if she saw Jesus' miracles or if she knew his teaching. What is more likely is that she had heard stories from her servants as they discussed the news spreading throughout Jerusalem. As she went to bed that night, chances are her head was full of questions and doubts and hopes as a result of all she had been hearing. A fertile ground for a message from the God and Father of the one who would stand before her husband that very day. When she awoke, eyes wide with fear and awe, she did not discount the disturbing dream and turbulent sleep she had experienced. She realized that whatever she had dreamed was not your ordinary, I-can't-believe-I-ate-the-whole-thing type of dream.

From Comfort to Conviction

"Have nothing to do with that *innocent* man," was her plea. Understandable, perhaps, if it were coming from one of Jesus' disciples; but what makes this statement incredible is that it was uttered by someone who had seen Jesus from a distance, if at all. This lady was Roman nobility itself. She had the best of everything first-century life had to offer: clothing, jewels, food, recreation, comfort. She had not been raised to protect the rights of the unfortunate. She had, in fact, been raised to please herself.

One of her peers was Herodias, wife of Herod the Tetrarch, infamous as the woman who had John the Baptist beheaded. Hence, Pilate's wife lived in a world where truth was easily distorted. Her own husband, in talking with Jesus, even posed the question, "What is truth?" (John 18:38).

Her husband was not a spiritual man, but rather a man of political ambition. In all likelihood, he, like other Roman officials, looked upon the Jews with disdain and disrespect. It is quite a phenomenon that, in the midst of this atmosphere, Pilate's wife would have any convictions about goodness and justice. She was spiritually sensitive enough to know she had been in touch with the divine—the *real* divine.

From Conviction to Responsibility

Pilate's wife was convinced of Jesus' innocence and in a swift and bold action, she sent an urgent message to her husband as Jesus stood before him to be judged. She knew Jesus was innocent, and the thought of his impending death haunted her. She also wanted to protect Pilate from being involved in the evil plan to kill him. She was probably fearful of what would happen to her husband and to herself if he were party to this man's death. If the dream itself caused her to suffer, how much more would she suffer if the dream became reality? Surely she would reason that the one who was powerful enough to send the dream was powerful enough to bring punishment if the innocent one died.

Unfortunately, Pilate did not have his wife's grasp of the spiritual implications of the event. Although he tried to talk the Jews out of having Jesus killed, he was not convinced by his wife's note to stand his ground and risk the accusation that he was disloyal to Caesar. Tradition tells us that Pilate's political downfall came shortly after Jesus' crucifixion—he was removed from office and banished to another country where he eventually committed suicide.[2]

From Responsibility to Courage

The culmination of this woman's conviction and sense of responsibility were fueled by her courage. No other person came to Jesus' defense at the time of his trial and crucifixion. Given the status of women at this time, it is likely that they did not often interfere or offer advice on judicial matters. Her interrupting the governor when he was "sitting on the judge's seat" was probably not a common occurrence. He must have been shocked when he received the message from the guard. In fact, he hesitated. He again gave the crowd an opportunity to release Jesus, but evil prevailed that day. He tried to rid himself of guilt by washing his hands in front of the mob, saying, "I am innocent of this man's blood. It is your responsibility" (Matthew 27:24). But the blood of Jesus Christ is not easily washed off the hands or hearts of men. Pilate's ritual and response was of no avail in saving his soul.

In the face of the angry mobs screaming, "Crucify him!" this woman dared to proclaim Jesus' innocence. As the governor's wife, she risked everything by going against the opinions of the Roman and

[2] Deen 208.

Jewish leaders. Incredibly, she became his *sole* defender that day. Her husband was unwilling to battle the crowds, and though he doubted Jesus' guilt, his desire to please the people won over his sense of justice and responsibility. On a day when darkest evil prevailed, Pilate's wife will always be known as a woman who spoke truth. Her husband asked, "What is truth?" She knew *who* was truth.

A Woman of Conviction

The wonder of the Scriptures. A Roman governor's wife who lived 2,000 years ago sent a message to her husband and speaks to my heart today. Before this month, I had skimmed over that little verse in Matthew many times, but never realized what I could learn from this woman.

Like Pilate's wife and many of her peers, I grew up selfish and spoiled, a people-pleaser who lacked strong opinions. Time after time, people urged me to stand up for what is right and to be a woman of deep conviction. Like this first-century woman, I finally *woke up* to truth—I have come to believe deeply that as Christians we must firmly hold to what the Bible says and never let sin become acceptable. I can think of times, even as a Christian, when I have lost perspective and become wishy-washy about right and wrong. My sin and the sin of others became hard to recognize. My focus again became pleasing people and not pleasing God. Even though I have been a Christian for a long time, I must always keep the word of God on my mind and heart. Without it, I can become like Pilate—convictionless and apt to make grave mistakes!

I believe that courage to act in accordance with conviction is crucial to my spiritual growth. When faced with responsibility, my nature is to shrink back and let feelings of insecurity control me. When this happens, I lose confidence and doubt that I can make a difference. As a Christian, and especially as a leader, that is not acceptable. I cannot help people go to heaven or grow as Christians when I shrink back and become insecure. I must be 100% responsible for those I lead.

My husband is a very powerful, aggressive leader. He naturally assumes complete responsibility for everything under his charge. During our early years in the ministry, it was easy to sit back and be quiet because he was such a dominant leader! I did not enjoy the ministry because I had not put my whole heart into it. I know now that he needs my input and that, in this way, I am truly supporting him. I have learned to give my heart to people and feel responsible for them. Accepting responsibility means that if you believe it, say it (wisely), and if you feel it, express it (appropriately). You may make some mistakes, and could possibly have conflicts with people, but you will learn and grow in your character. Being supportive of your husband or leaders in the church means saying what you believe with conviction.

Pilate's wife was a courageous woman in that she did what she could to save Jesus. In the same way, I am inspired by the courage of those in the kingdom who have remained faithful in the face of disappointments and discouragement. I have battled with wanting to quit, being resentful towards God, and being selfish with my time, life and family. The courage to face sin, challenges and failure can only come from God and the Bible. The answer is always to live by faith and to trust God. He was able to use Pilate's wife to testify to Jesus' innocence because of her deep conviction, her sense of responsibility and her courage. As I continue to grow in these areas, there is nothing more exciting than knowing that God is using me to make the kingdom grow!

Cathy Marutzky
Los Angeles, USA

 FOCUS Is truth easy for you to recognize, or has it become blurred in your life? Would people say you are a woman of conviction?

application questions on page 179

17

SAPPHIRA
The Fruit of Deception

Acts 5:1-11

The things that angels longed to see were unfolding (1 Peter 1:12). Jesus, the Son of God, had come in the flesh, had lived out the very nature of God, and had died for the sins of Jew and Gentile alike. Only a few months earlier, he had been raised in glory to return to his Father, allowing the outpouring of the gift of his continuing presence—the Holy Spirit. The day of Pentecost ushered in a whole new order, the *church* of Jesus Christ. A group of 3,000 Jews came to believe that the Messiah truly had come to open the way to God; they had become disciples and were sharing their hearts, lives and possessions in celebration of their new oneness with the God of their Fathers (Acts 2:42-47). The message spread throughout Jerusalem, and God added 2,000 more to their number. The disciples sacrificed to meet the needs manifested in such a large group. A fertile ground for the growth of generosity...and deception.

◆

First century A.D.—truly an exciting time to be alive! Ananias and Sapphira were a privileged couple. They had the opportunity to witness firsthand the beginnings of the early church. They experienced the royal growth of the kingdom. They saw the daily evangelism and the radical sacrifice of the disciples. Not only did they see God at work, they were an integral part of it.

An Unclean Heart

"What a sacrificial brother, Joseph the Levite!" All day Sapphira had been hearing the news. Joseph had become the talk of the church. He had sold a piece of property and had given it to the apostles to use for the needs of the church (Acts 4: 32-37).

Instead of being inspired by Joseph's example, Sapphira felt depressed, angry, trapped. Why did Joseph have to spoil things for her? She and

Ananias had also decided to sell a piece of their property (Acts 5: 1). They had great plans for the money—new clothes, better tools for Ananias, and a long-awaited holiday to Rome—all things were desperately needed. They had been working hard for the kingdom and deserved a break.

Sapphira remembered that last week an announcement was made to the assembly. There was a great need for money to support the spreading of the gospel into Judea and Samaria and to help the Grecian widows. Ananias had mentioned possibly giving part of the money they received for the property. She had hoped that he would forget. She felt sorry for the widows, but she still wanted her holiday. She didn't want it shortened or to have to stay at the disciples' houses. A luxurious room in an inn sounded so nice. Greed and self indulgence began to grip her heart.

The Battles Within

"What a sacrifice he made!" The words said about Joseph were once said about Ananias and Sapphira. As young Christians, they were completely sold out for Jesus. Knowing the heart and life-style of Jesus and seeing the apostles' lives inspired them to be radical and sacrificial. The battle between pleasing God and pleasing self became easy. God was first; self was last. Position and comfort didn't matter—only the souls of mankind. The needs were so obvious—physically, emotionally and spiritually. Most of the first 3,000 converts were not from Jerusalem—they had no place to stay, no jobs, no families, no food. Even though about 10,000 were saved, there were still so many souls waiting for the gospel to reach them. Sacrifice had been the hearts of Ananias and Sapphira...until now.

Lately, every call for sacrifice caused a tug in Sapphira's heart. Her old self (Ephesians 4:20-24) was resurrecting. Things and comfort began to matter too much. There became a battle inside her heart—righteousness before God or sin with the god of self. Whom would she please?

As Sapphira wrestled in her heart, another battle began to take place. What will people expect of her? Sapphira knew that the entire church had heard about Joseph. They knew that Ananias was selling his property as well. The expectation would be for Ananias and Sapphira to do the same. That was their reputation.

Pressured. Burdened. Trapped. What choice did they really have? Not to give would signify selfishness, greed and materialism. To give would mean giving up the desires of her heart. A lose-lose situation. What would people think? Respect or condemnation?

No longer was it an inward battle for righteousness. Instead it had become an outward battle for preservation—preservation of status, position and reputation.

Fear of Exposure

Ananias and Sapphira faced a major decision—the most difficult decision so far in their Christian walk. This decision would ultimately determine the course of their lives. The battles were many. Their many priorities were cluttered. The pressure was enormous. There was no clear-cut choice. So what should they do? How could they determine what was best?

Help! Inside, Ananias and Sapphira must have felt the cry for help screaming through their heads and their hearts. Outwardly, however, their lips were silent. Help was available. The apostles were still in Jerusalem. They had not yet been scattered because of persecution. Other disciples were facing similar choices. Ananias and Sapphira were not alone in their struggle. They had many friends who could have helped. But they chose to do it alone.

Ananias and Sapphira desperately needed input. The world teaches survival of the prideful and independent. God teaches that victory is only sure with many advisors (Proverbs 11:14). Getting advice requires openness and exposure. That scares us! Ananias and Sapphira feared people knowing the *real* Ananias and Sapphira who had self-indulgence and greed in their hearts.

They forgot that when they had become disciples they were totally exposed. They had always been exposed before God (Hebrews 4:12-13). For the first time, they were exposed to people. It was a freeing time. Exposure to other people brought the necessary ingredient to radically change—humility (James 4:6-10). They made changes that were incredible. As older Christians, Ananias and Sapphira still needed to continually purify their unclean hearts through openness and the blood of Jesus in order to make radical changes and right choices (1 John 1:5-10).

It had become easy for Sapphira to be 100% open with Ananias. Being open with others was much more challenging. Since they both were struggling to overcome the sins in their hearts, Ananias and Sapphira needed outside help. Whether Sapphira saw the need to get help, we're not certain. Whether she was aware or not, she did not pursue it. Instead Ananias and Sapphira wrestled to the point of decision on their own.

Destroyed by Deceit

Ananias and Sapphira devised their plan. They wanted it all—the money for themselves, the ability to sacrifice for the church, and the reputation of being a model couple. They were willing to do anything to achieve it. So they "kept back part of the money for themselves, but brought the rest and put it at the apostles' feet" (Acts 5:2), fully knowing that the apostles and the rest of the church would assume that all the money was given. But they forgot the power of the Holy Spirit to reveal the truth.

God did indeed use them as a model couple for the entire church—a negative model. God will not be mocked. He confronted Ananias with his sin, and then struck him dead on the spot. God then gave Sapphira a chance to be open. If Sapphira had not known about Ananias' plan or was repentant about her deception, in all likelihood God would have allowed her to live. We too, like Sapphira, are responsible for our own sins. Sapphira, however, because of her selfishness, chose to lie to God and to his church. She allowed her heart to become hardened by sin and its deceitfulness (Hebrews 3:13-18). As a result, Sapphira lost her life—physically and spiritually.

Hardened by Sin's Deceitfulness

Sapphira moved from being privileged, sacrificial and responsible to being selfish, prideful and deceptive. That's a description of my fourteen years as a Christian. In the beginning, I started my Christian walk just like Sapphira. I, too, was privileged to witness the beginnings of a worldwide movement of disciples who were committed to God, the Bible and the lost world. I saw the daily evangelism and radical sacrifice of the disciples, and I was amazed. I wanted to be just like them! I remember as a teen and a college student at M.I.T. being so excited to sacrifice time, energy and money to help souls become Christians and to see mission teams sent to Chicago, London, New York.

I wanted to grow and become a leader—not out of a desire for position, but simply out of a desire to meet needs. I became a leader in college, and when I graduated, I was asked to go into the full-time ministry. What a dream come true!

Years later, however, after being in the full-time ministry and even becoming a single woman's ministry leader, selfishness, greed and pride began creeping into my heart. I started fighting the battle for my rights, privileges and position rather than the battle for righteousness before God. I wanted so many things—to lead my own sector, to have more financial security, to be married and to be on a mission team. Everything was focused on *me*. Attitudes started developing in my heart. As a result, I began to give less of my heart, but I was still held up as a loving person. I began to sacrifice less, but still more than most, so everyone would still think I was sacrificial.

Inside, I was doomed to destruction. No one knew how I felt. No one knew the many battles I was fighting inside. I was too prideful to let people in. I wanted to be the model Christian, but my heart was becoming hard.

I thank God for the power of the Word and Christian friends. This past year, I began opening up my ugly, unclean heart to Anita and Jimmy Allen. It occurred in many stages. It took honesty—gut-level honesty—to expose the deeply imbedded selfishness, greed and pride that needed to be confronted. My inward battle became a *right* battle—a battle for my heart, not for my position and my reputation. This past summer, I finally broke through and overcame my sin. I desperately needed the help of friends and leaders in my life. Without them, I would still be trapped and doomed to destruction.

Righteousness before God is an ongoing battle. I have learned that humility and honesty are necessary to win the battles every day.

Joyce (Lee) Tan
Singapore

 FOCUS

What battles are you fighting in your heart? Are you more concerned about your heart or your reputation? With whom are you being gut-level honest?

application questions on page 179

18

MARY, MOTHER OF JOHN MARK
A Giving Heart

Acts 12:1-19

Hospitality was the hallmark of Jewish society. Rabbis thought it more important than attending early morning academies of learning—quite a priority since Jews placed such a high value on studying. A Jewish believer, Mary, the mother of John Mark, gave hospitality a deeper meaning. During a period of intense persecution against the disciples, she continued to offer her home as a gathering place. Some have even suggested that the Pentecost event of Acts 2 might have taken place there. Obviously a woman of means and seemingly a widow, she risked her reputation and life for the sake of the church.

In all likelihood, her home was on the south end of the western hill of Mount Zion, which was a residential section of Jerusalem. The disciples would have walked along the white stone pavement to come to her house, a place of refuge.

◆

"Alone! I feel so totally and terribly alone. How will I ever make it? It's not right! A child needs both a mother and a father. A young boy needs a man to talk to, to look up to and to learn from. I can't do it!"

Knowing human nature, we can be relatively sure that some thoughts of this sort went through the mind of Mary since she was most likely a widow and a single mother. It seems that she was left with a large house and a fairly comfortable inheritance. She was also left with a young son named John Mark. As a single mother, it would have been easy to fall into self-pity or despair. Perhaps she did. But somewhere along the line she met another man, who changed the entire course of her life.

A Disciple of Jesus

It is quite likely that Mary met Jesus before he died and began to follow him. When Jesus sent the disciples to prepare for the Passover feast and his last supper, he sent them into Jerusalem to a home where he even referred to the upstairs room as "my guest room" (Mark 14:12-15). Could that have been Mary's house? Had she already begun to give what she had to give to Jesus—her home, her food, her hospitality? If so, John Mark must have loved it when Jesus and the others were there with all the laughter and joking, as well as stimulating spiritual conversation. He probably would have especially liked the big, outgoing fisherman named Peter. Most likely, the whole room seemed to come alive when Peter walked in—he was so full of life.

If it was Mary's home in which the Last Supper was eaten, what an impression that must have made on the young John Mark as he watched Jesus and the Twelve eating that last meal together! I can almost see him standing off to the side as his mother served and as the disciples spent their last hours together.

He must have realized that there was something different as the thirteen men ate that Passover meal together. They were quieter, and they seemed sad and worried. When they left, I wonder if John Mark followed them all the way to the Mount of Olives? Did he watch Jesus weep and pray all night? Why was Jesus, who was always so strong, confident and joyful, now in such despair? He couldn't have known or understood; it would have scared him.

Since the Gospel of Mark is the only account that speaks of a young man running away from would-be captors that night in the garden, and since John Mark wrote that gospel, many assume that John Mark himself was the young man. If so, he would never have forgotten what happened. It was probably one of the most frightening moments of his life, and surely it became the most embarrassing. In all the confusion surrounding Jesus' arrest, they seized John Mark as well. In a panic, John Mark wriggled away from his captors and slipped right out of his clothes. He ran home completely naked! As a mother, we can only imagine the shocked expression on Mary's face as her son crept into the house, naked and ashamed.

Kingdom As Family

From those early days and throughout his life, Peter and John Mark developed a very special relationship. In 1 Peter 5:13, the apostle refers to him as "my son Mark." It seems that Peter became the father he didn't have. After Jesus left this world, John Mark must have sat for hours while Peter told him all he could remember about his days with the

Master. He hung on every word Peter said, every memory he recalled; it was as if he had been there himself. The gospel he later wrote surely is the result of the experiences Peter shared with him.

Mary watched her young son, and her heart almost broke and sang at the same time as she saw the love and devotion that Peter and John Mark had for one another. God was so good. He had given her a family and her son a father. As for Mary, she became known for her generosity and hospitality. Her home was always open, and disciples gathered regularly at her house for prayer, worship and fellowship. A house full of people meant a lot of extra work, but would Mary have traded it for peace and quiet? Not for a minute. She and her son were part of something great and powerful.

'It's Peter'

In the early days of the church, there was one night in particular that Mary could never forget. Peter was in prison—again—but this time seemed as if it would be the last. He was being guarded not just by the usual one or two men, but by a continual rotation of four armed soldiers, and his trial was scheduled for the next day. James had already been beheaded; Peter would certainly be next. The disciples had suffered through great persecution and hardships before, but to lose two of their strongest and most beloved leaders at once was almost more than they could bear.

One by one, they gathered at Mary's house and began to pray fervently for the life of their leader and friend. God heard those prayers and answered quickly and powerfully. When an angel was sent to release Peter from prison, his chains were broken and Peter was led, unharmed, past all the guards and out of the prison.

Immediately he rushed to Mary's house. When Mary's servant girl, Rhoda, answered Peter's knock at the door, she was so astounded that in her excitement she left him standing outside. She ran in to tell Mary and the others, but no one would believe her. "It can't be Peter," they told her, "You're crazy. Now be quiet so we can finish praying for Peter!" But then they heard more knocks at the door, this time louder and more insistent. "Rhoda!" a voice whispered, "Let me in! Rhoda!"

The disciples' eyes widened and they all rushed to the door, hearts pounding. Imagine their reactions when they saw Peter on the doorstep. "Stop standing there gaping!" He must have cried, laughing,

"Let me in before someone sees me!" Mary, John Mark and the other disciples must have laughed often as they remembered that night. Never had they been more urgent in their prayers and yet so faithless in their expectation: how humbling and how embarrassing, how amazing and how just plain funny!

Time to Let Go

It was several years later that Mary was faced with what every mother eventually must face: the time to let go of her son. She had met Paul (Saul then) a few years earlier when her nephew Barnabus had brought him to her house. She was afraid at first. But Saul was the most zealous disciple Mary had ever met. His intensity and his determination to tell the world about Jesus must have challenged and convicted Mary to the core of her being. Over the next few years, John Mark grew up and his relationship with Paul also grew.

Mary must have been both proud and petrified when Paul extended the invitation to John Mark to accompany him on his next missionary journey (Acts 12:25). Mary must have wept as she said good-bye to her only son, knowing she might never see him again. It must have seemed so quiet when John Mark was gone; life must have seemed so different. And yet, as Mary found out, the job of a mother is never truly over. As hard as it was for Mary to say good-bye to John Mark, I wonder how much harder it must have been when he came home hurt, discouraged and feeling like a failure. Traveling with Paul was a great opportunity but it was not for the faint-hearted. John Mark did not get very far before he turned back.

Probably the most difficult time of all came for Mary when Paul refused to allow John Mark to accompany him on his next missionary trip (Acts 15:36-40). He had not proven strong; he had not proven reliable; he could not be trusted.

What was Mary's response? Did she get upset with Paul, or did she see that God's hand was refining her pampered son? All we know is that Mary's son did grow and did become strong. So much so that years later, when Paul was in prison and facing death, he sent for John Mark, knowing that while others had deserted him, John Mark would not (2 Timothy 4:11).

Leaving a Legacy

Mary's story is that of a mother and a young man. She thought she would have to raise her son alone, but God provided what she did not have: a family. He gave John Mark spiritual fathers and brothers and sisters, as well as aunts, uncles, grandparents and life-long friends. He had Peter, who remained his father in the faith throughout his life. He had Barnabus, his cousin, who became a special older brother and mentor who believed in him when he was young and immature and struggling spiritually.

Because of her generosity and her faithfulness, Mary's son did more than she ever could have. He grew from a curious but timid young boy to become a valuable companion and helper to God's greatest evangelizers and then went on to reliably record God's account of Jesus himself by writing the Gospel of Mark, the earliest account of Jesus' life.

Worthy of Imitation

My study of Mary was like embarking on an exciting scavenger hunt! I began with one clue (Acts 12:12), but the more closely I looked, the more information I realized I had been given! The one clue that I began with led me to countless others, and at the end of the journey I discovered a priceless treasure! I came to love and appreciate God's word more than ever before. The more deeply I examine it, the more there is to discover and to learn.

The first thing that profoundly impacted me as I studied Mary was the fact that she was a single mother. I know how difficult it was for her and how hard it is for all single mothers to provide not only physically and emotionally for their children, but also to grow spiritually themselves.

Mary is a powerful example of God's plan to set the lonely in families (Psalm 68:6). Look at the strong male influences that God provided for Mary's son: Peter, Barnabus and Paul, to name a few. Yet the blessings God provided for Mary would never have been possible had she not given all she had and all she could to God and his kingdom. She was not a weak, needy woman standing on the fringes of the fellowship, waiting for her needs to be met or her loneliness to be taken away. She was a strong, vibrant part of God's great family.

Seeing the outcome of my (physical) sister's life in the kingdom has brought me great joy. She became a disciple shortly after her divorce and raised three children as a single mother. Her children had some incredible men who became spiritual fathers and brothers to them, and all three of them are now grown and are strong disciples. My sister has grown to become a powerful and very fruitful Christian, a grateful mother and now, years later, a godly wife! God does set the lonely in families.

I also was extremely challenged and inspired by Mary's unselfish hospitality. The one gospel fact we have is that she gave her house to be used for the kingdom. I have a husband, four children, one dog and two cats and, honestly, just running my household—keeping it somewhat clean, keeping food in the house and getting the laundry done—as well as leading the women's ministry, is a big job! I like things to be fairly orderly, and I really enjoy peace and calm. I realize this doesn't mesh too well with the life of a big family and the ministry. Therein is my lesson to be learned from Mary. She gave so unselfishly—her home, her food and her "space." I am sure she got back a dirty house, an empty pantry and a lot of confusion, but she also received so much more: relationships! I wouldn't trade what my children have from being raised in the midst of the kingdom for anything. The people that come through my house have become great influences in their lives, their most special friends and most inspiring examples. Mary's life challenges me to keep serving and not to pull back, become selfish or to protect "my space."

Mary also gives me a tremendous sense of gratitude for the kingdom of God. Being raised in the kingdom from the time they were very young has given my children a spiritual start in life that is priceless. They have been around spiritual giants in the faith. They have heard their stories; they know their lives; and they are imitating their examples and convictions. Because of what they have seen and heard it would be difficult for any of them to leave God or his kingdom. It is real—they have seen it in the lives all around them.

I am most moved by Mary as a mother who had to watch her son grow up and leave. I can so relate to all she must have gone through as she "cut the apron strings" and gave him the freedom to follow his own dreams and live his own life. I *hurt* with her as she saw him suffer and fail, and go through his own conflicts and rejection, and I wanted to cheer with her as he came through his struggles, solid and strong. The greatest joy for parents is to see their children grow to become strong men and women who love God and his kingdom. And yet, that is accomplished with a heartache of its own. Not only do we miss them emotionally, but now we face something else: the challenge of trusting other disciples to love them and disciple them. I remember how grateful I was to have the help of other people in my daughter's life, but I must admit that it tested me and my own faith! I know that as a mother, I will *always* have a special place in my children's lives but I have to step aside now and let others help them. What a special gift Mary has been to my life. I pray fervently that I, like Mary, will leave behind a life and a legacy that touches others for eternity.

Geri Laing
Chapel Hill, North Carolina, USA

 Are you known as a giver? Do you freely offer hospitality—even when it is inconvenient?

application questions on page 180

19

RHODA

Opportunity Knocks

Acts 12:1-19

During the first century, the church was comprised of both slaves and owners, servants and employers, poor and prominent. Whole households, as in the case of Lydia, accepted Jesus as Lord. It would seem that Mary, the mother of Mark, and at least one of her household servants, Rhoda, were bonded in such a way. They had each embraced and accepted the forgiving sacrifice of Jesus, and along with other believers, they gathered in the house to pray for Peter's release from prison. The blood of Jesus flowed through boundaries erected by the surrounding culture, and the believers in Jerusalem and elsewhere became one in spirit and purpose.

◆

Mary's home was an oasis for the disciples in Jerusalem. The apostles were in and out, and Rhoda, her servant, had abundant opportunities to serve. Although Rhoda was welcomed as a sister, she knew that her place was still to serve. That is what Jesus would have done, and Rhoda wanted to be like him in every way. Legally she belonged to Mary; spiritually she belonged to Jesus—two reasons to give her best.

Life in the Kingdom

She was so excited when the disciples gathered in the upper room, talking about the struggles and victories of life in the kingdom. She loved most of all to hear them pray; she felt so small on her own, but as she joined them in prayer, she could feel her faith and trust in God grow. She knew God would honor their prayers to make a difference in the lost world, to bring the disciples to complete unity, to protect them from the evil one.

Her faith was built as she heard the stories of Jesus told by the apostles. She learned so much by listening to how Jesus responded

116

to the poor, the Pharisees, the woman at the well. These men had been with Jesus, and they laughed at how different they were from when they had first met him. Rhoda laughed, too, and was encouraged that she could also be different. She set her goals: confident, persistent, trusting. She knew she needed to grow quickly, because life in the kingdom was dangerous. James had just been beheaded, and now Peter was in prison.

Late-Night Prayer Session

That night there was a prayer meeting at Mary's house; all the disciples prayed for Peter's life to be spared. Rhoda was busy, but added her own silent prayers as she moved in and out of the room, taking coats and helping the little ones settle down to sleep. It fell to her to open the door since she knew all of the disciples, and could keep out anyone wanting to *prey* rather than pray. Most everyone had already arrived, so she was on her guard when she went to the door late that night.

What? That voice...it was Peter!! God had answered their prayers, her prayers, so quickly! She was filled with joy and burst into the prayer meeting, "Stop praying! God has been listening! Peter is here!" Rhoda was so convinced that God had brought Peter to them that she was not even distracted by the apostles unbelief, but kept insisting to them that it was true! What boldness! She wasn't offended that they didn't believe her; she realized with her simple faith that it wasn't that they didn't trust *her*, but that they didn't trust *God*. She didn't get defensive and take their unbelief personally, but kept pointing them to God.

God could have allowed Peter to walk right into the room—he had just allowed him to walk out of jail. Perhaps God wanted the disciples to experience an answer to prayer through the simple, but resolute, faith of a servant girl. They prayed and doubted, but Rhoda prayed and believed.

Healing Through Giving

After spending many days with young Rhoda, I have gotten the sense that she was a woman of great faith. Her home life provided a tremendously strong foundation. Being intimately involved with

Mary's life, day-in and day-out, would have given her a picture of the kingdom that she never would have gotten if she had lived in her own small home in another section of Jerusalem. No doubt, she witnessed many answered prayers—Peter's release being only one of them.

There is nothing more rewarding than watching your prayers be answered, but I have had to learn that my prayers are answered on God's timetable and not mine. I have also had to learn that God's *delays* are not *denials*.

I prayed diligently to have children. Month after month, year after year, my prayers were not answered. Little did I know that God was preparing me to totally and utterly depend on his sovereign rule in my life. After four-and-a-half years of praying and struggling with my faith, wondering if God really cared about me, I became pregnant—not with one baby, but with twins! Ron and I were totally amazed and shocked and then remembered that we had originally prayed for twins. Everything went well and there were no complications during the pregnancy or delivery. Jonathan and Joshua were born on November 29, 1990, in Johannesburg, South Africa.

While in the hospital, Joshua contracted a respiratory virus and pneumonia, and since he was three weeks premature, his lungs were too weak to cope. At 17 days old, the Lord took Joshua to be with him. My greatest test of faith to date...*would I pass?* What else could I do but trust that God could get me through this most painful time of my life? I had to remember that early in my pregnancy I had prayed that God could do whatever he needed to do with my children, whatever would help their lives have the most impact.

We buried Joshua in Syracuse, New York, my husband's home town. As a result of our talking with a friend during this time, he promised us that a church would be planted there. The church now is growing and many souls are being saved. Joshua's life and death is having impact on many.

After Joshua's death, there was a need for us to move back to the U.S. to lead the church in Chicago. I had to dig down deep inside myself, and pray and trust that God would use me despite the spiritual and emotional pain I was feeling. Just as Rhoda had to give of herself during a difficult time for the church, so God was calling me to give of myself and serve during this difficult time in my life. I knew, deep down, that one of the best ways for me to get over the pain of losing Joshua and leaving behind some of my best friends in South Africa was immediately to give my heart and my life to the disciples in Chicago.

Just as Rhoda heard the voice of Peter and knew her prayers were answered, I look into the faces of my brothers and sisters in the Midwest, and I know that God answered my prayer in helping me give away my hurting heart.

Lavonia Drabot
Charlotte, North Carolina, USA

 How much do you believe when you pray? Do you expect answers, or are you amazed when they come?

application questions on page 180

20

SALOME
MOTHER OF JAMES AND JOHN
True Greatness

Matthew 20:20-28; 27:55-56; Mark 16:1-8

"Land of Zebulun and land of Naphtali,
  the way to the sea, along the Jordan,
Galilee of the Gentiles
  the people living in darkness have seen a great light;
on those living in the land of the shadow of death
  a light has dawned" (Matthew 4:15-16).

Jesus grew up about 20 miles from the Sea of Galilee. Surely he was no stranger to the lush, almost tropical shoreline and the refreshing sea air. It was on those shores he called his first four apostles, men who were ready to drop their nets and follow him to do some spiritual fishing. He said to them, "...I will make you fishers of men."

How fitting of Jesus to begin his ministry in Galilee, far from the academies of Judea, far from the inside rabbinic track. The statement of Nathaniel summed up the prejudices of the time: "Can anything good come out of Nazareth?" But the son of a country carpenter was more than he appeared.

Two of the fishermen he called, James and John, left their nets with their father, Zebedee, and the hired men. They walked away from the family and the lake that had sustained and supported them. They followed an itinerant, untrained *rabbi,* not knowing where he would take them, but knowing that they must go.

◆

Salome—not the dancer who enticed Herod, resulting in the death of John the Baptist. But Salome, the mother of James and John, the two close friends of Jesus. Until Jesus walked into their lives and hearts, the boys had worked side by side with their father, Zebedee, in the family fishing business. Owning several boats and having hired hands, the family must have been relatively well-to-do and influential in the community.

Whether Zebedee himself became a follower of Jesus is unclear, but his wife was one of the women who followed Jesus to the very end—to Jerusalem and to the cross. Mark tells us that she even accompanied Mary Magdalene on her trip to the tomb to anoint the body which was not to be found. She surely witnessed the miracle of all miracles—the resurrected Christ.

Like all followers of Jesus, along the way she had some lessons to learn as she took on the heart of the one she followed.

Ambitious

Salome was the mother of two of the three disciples in Jesus' inner circle—Peter being the third. Jesus chose them to accompany him during the most memorable and decisive times of his ministry. They were on the mountain with him, witnessing his stunning transfiguration and his conversation with the long dead prophets Moses and Elijah (Matthew 17:1-8). They were allowed in the room with him when he raised Jairus' daughter from the dead (Mark 5:21-43). During his most difficult hour in Gethsemane, he took them with him, away from the others, and poured out his heart to them, beseeching their prayers (Mark 14:32-42).

Salome must have been very thankful that her boys enjoyed such a place of honor in their friendship with Jesus. But in such situations, a thankful heart can become prideful and filled with worldly ambition. Jesus knew that in his ministry he needed particularly to focus on a few and transfer his heart to them on a day-to-day basis. The three he chose were not necessarily *better* than the others; they were simply *chosen*.

Salome, however, was very ambitious and wanted even more prestige for James and John. Toward the end of Jesus' ministry she made a public request of him. Kneeling before him she said, "Grant that one of these two sons of mine may sit at your right and the other at your left in your kingdom" (Matthew 20:21). Many thoughts must have flooded her mind before she made this request. Jesus had spoken of his death, but more importantly, of his resurrection. She could have thought that he would rise from the dead to return and establish his powerful kingdom on earth, and she wanted her sons to have a place beside the throne. Possibly she felt their only real rival for either of the honored positions was Peter. *Obviously Jesus would choose two of the three to be with him.* And Peter was so outspoken…maybe she wanted to beat him to it. Whatever her reasoning, she was very bold to make this request and surely felt confident that Jesus would grant it. *After all, I have sacrificed a lot of things for the master.* She saw the window of opportunity for her sons to be successful and influential in this new kingdom.

Salome was focused on the worldly prestige rather than the spiritual condition of her sons. Perhaps that is why Jesus denied her request. However, we can all be challenged by how her ambition led her to take such a risk. Godly ambition and the willingness to take chances bring out the best in us and in those around us. Salome's ambition and passion were transferred into the hearts of her sons, one who would become the best-loved follower of Jesus, and the other who would later be the first apostle martyred for his Lord.

Discipled

Jesus, wise as he was, answered this eager mother and her two sons, "You will indeed drink from my cup, but to sit at my right or left is not for me to grant. These places belong to those for whom they have been prepared by my Father" (Matthew 20:23). We might imagine that the other 10 disciples were eager for these places as well and may have wished their own mothers would be so bold. Salome was discipled by Jesus and needed his gentle rebuke to learn that true greatness was not something that could be earned, but only gained through sacrifice. Jesus made it clear who is the greatest: "Whoever wants to be great among you must be your servant, and whoever wants to be first must be your slave—just as the Son of Man did not come to be served, but to serve, and to give his life as a ransom for many" (Matthew 20:26-28). We get confused and think that true greatness is seen in how we prove ourselves or in the achievements we count so worthy. Jesus, who was truly great, blazed the trail to greatness by laying down his life for others.

Salome had definitely been put in her place. Perhaps she was embarrassed and may have regretted making the request. Nevertheless, her heart and her motives were exposed, and she accepted the discipling she received from Jesus. It is evident that she felt secure with Jesus since she came before him asking a favor. It is also evident that she continued to remain secure in his love as we see her continuing to follow him. Surely she had seen Jesus correct and rebuke others, and she herself had probably already felt the stings of correction from the Master. Bold and willing to take correction, she remained a faithful follower to the end.

Committed

Salome had experienced much in her life since James and John dropped their nets to follow Jesus. She and Zebedee had to take up the slack created by the loss of their sons in the business. Those who did not accept the claims or support the ministry of Jesus must have given Zebedee and Salome a rough time: *How could your sons just go off and leave you like this? Don't they love you? Is being a fisherman not good enough or spiritual enough for them?* She must have gone through times of fear and anxiety as she watched her sons give up all they had to follow this radical Jesus. Yet Salome worked through any concerns or doubts she may have had; she was humble enough to learn from her own children, and she herself followed the Teacher from Galilee.

Along with other women she helped support Jesus out of her means and cared for his needs. She bonded with these women, one being Mary the mother of Jesus. They must have talked, as mothers do, of their sons' futures, the hopes and dreams they had for them. Yes, and the fears. Just as Mary physically outlived her son, Salome may have outlived James who was beheaded by Herod Agrippa, while John was exiled to the Island of Patmos. Mothers of the truly great have much to ponder in their hearts as they suffer with their righteous children.

We see the quality of commitment in Salome's life through her relationships. She was committed to James and John, wanting the best for them and supporting them as they followed the dictates of their hearts at the expense of the family business. At the cross, Jesus entrusted his own mother to John. Could it be that Jesus saw the commitment John had to *his* mother, and therefore, chose him to care for his own mother?

Salome was committed not only to Jesus, but to Mary as well, as Salome stood beside her at the cross, grieving the death of her firstborn. She did not distance herself out of the fear that she and her sons might suffer in a similar scene as a direct result of their association with Jesus (Mark 15:40).

It was her total, unflinching commitment to Jesus that kept such an ambitious woman faithful through the disappointment and embarrassment of being denied her request before Jesus. Sometimes we can feel as if God does not give us what we want or that he is not with us. Often we battle with anger, self-pity and resentment when we do not get our way. Yet because Salome knew Jesus, she didn't allow *not getting her own way* to cause her to give up on her commitment to him.

As women who profess to follow Jesus, let us learn from Salome's example and grow in our ambition and in our willingness to let our hearts be discipled without giving in to fear, discouragement and bitterness. Let us renew our commitment to our faithful Creator, no matter the cost of true greatness.

Convicted

Salome challenges my spirituality as a mother, causing me to be much more aware of my children's most important needs—their spiritual ones. As a mother of four boys and one girl, ages seven to 14, I can often be more concerned with the worldly needs of my children's lives and neglect their spiritual needs. This usually happens when I am overwhelmed by the pressures of daily life and put my trust in things other than God. When I am in this muddled state, I do not allow him to work in my life the way he would like to.

In the past year and a half, we've been in four different churches in four major cities in the U.S. As we have sought first the kingdom, our moves have taken us across the country and, at times, into very spiritually challenging situations. As you can imagine, there have been times when my thoughts have been controlled by fear and anxiety. *How will my children adjust to this move? What will the new school system be like? Will they make new friends quickly? Are they going to miss the old ones? Will there be a community basketball league there?* While it is imperative that we consider and meet needs as parents, we must allow ourselves to be taught by God not to fret, but rather, to trust. God is so faithful.

Meeting the physical needs of my five children is a demanding task, and I work hard at it. But over the past year and a half, I have been discipled by God as he has shown me that what is most important is providing a spiritual environment and heart so that my children will be secure. He has reminded me that by seeking his kingdom first, he will meet all of our physical needs—just as he promised. In every move we have made for the kingdom, our children have been blessed with many friends, good grades in school and great achievements in sports.

It is great to be a mother in God's kingdom and to have the examples of other families who have raised their children to be disciples. As my children get older, I can be oblivious to their sins. God continues to teach me through his Word, and through other women, to have greater discernment and to accept the truth about my children. I want to keep Salome's heart by responding to correction with gratefulness.

I must continually keep my focus on the spiritual well-being of my children. Sometimes I am more consumed with how "I" am doing as a parent and lose the focus on how my child is doing. What a self-focused response to look at *my* weaknesses and faults so much that I don't expend the spiritual energy to help my children change and grow in their weak areas.

I can imagine that Salome was tempted to gain self-esteem and confidence from her children's talents and accomplishments. As with most mothers, she could have allowed her children to become the focus of her life. Occasionally I realize that I am living through and for my children, and not for God. This leads to me being overprotective and overbearing with my children. I try to keep them from every hurt, every pain and every negative experience. In Salome, I see a mother willing to let her children take the necessary steps of faith and to experience the risk that following Jesus requires. Salome did not live *through* her children; she became a dedicated disciple and had serious spiritual ambition for her own life.

We must count the cost as Christian mothers. We must ambitiously seek what is spiritual, be open to discipling and keep a radical commitment to Jesus that will live as a legacy for our children and their children. May it ultimately be said of all of us that we, like Salome, stayed with Jesus to the very end.

Judy Weger
San Francisco, USA

 FOCUS Is your commitment to Jesus one that inspires and challenges your family and others? Are you more concerned with the worldly or spiritual needs of those around you?

application questions on page 181

21

DORCAS
An Open-Heart Policy

Acts 9:36-43

Much was made of mourning the dead in Jewish custom. Professional mourners and musicians were hired to enhance the grief-filled atmosphere. Devout Jews observed a prescribed mourning procedure which included the following:

◆ As long as the dead body was in the house, no food could be prepared or eaten and no wine could be drunk.
◆ If someone did need to eat in the home, he was to eat with his back to the body.
◆ The mourners, both personal and professional, were to tear their clothing (generally about a six-inch rip in the inner garment).
◆ For seven days *deep* mourning was to be observed, with the first three being devoted to weeping.
◆ The anniversary of the death was to be observed.

In an upper room in Joppa, a seacoast town 38 miles from Jerusalem, people were beginning the mourning process, that is, until a man called Peter called on his God—the God who was, and is, the author of life itself.

◆

Two thousand years ago, in the little town of Joppa, there was a funeral. Just like today, funerals were a part of life in Joppa. Mourners wailed; friends and relatives comforted each other; the rituals were performed; the body was prepared. Yet there was something very different about this funeral. The weeping was more intense; the tears were more sincere; the mourners' hearts were more broken. Someone really special had died, someone who would be missed by many. Her name was Dorcas. She was a disciple, and therefore, she was going to heaven. So why such intense grief? Because her life left a mark; it had an impact on so many people. She had quite a reputation in Joppa. When others talked about her, there were three things they would say. First of all, they'd say Dorcas had a heart that feels.

Heart That Feels

To Dorcas, being a disciple meant loving and serving others, taking care of their needs, and considering them better than herself. Acts 9:36 tells us that she was "always doing good and helping the poor." She would look at people in need, and her heart would go out to them. She could feel their problems, their hurts, their loneliness. She saw it as her mission in life to alleviate others' pain, to get down on her knees and serve. The account in Acts presents her as a selfless woman.

Dorcas understood the heart of Christianity. She did not get caught up in legalism, competitiveness or worldliness. Her religion was pure. As James writes, "Religion that God our Father accepts as pure and faultless is this: to look after orphans and widows in their distress and to keep oneself from being polluted by the world" (James 1:27). We cannot imagine Dorcas strutting around trying to impress people. She did not seek the seat of honor. She did not care if she was overlooked. She just wanted to serve.

Dorcas was a lot like Jesus. As a first-century disciple, she had taken on Jesus' mission of seeking and saving the lost. But she understood that the way to win people was to care for them and meet their needs—that included their physical needs. She knew that if she helped the poor and made them clothes, people would notice how different, how compassionate she was, and they would be drawn to Jesus. The same compassion that inspired her to meet physical needs also led her to meet spiritual needs.

It is so tempting for us in our fast-paced ministries to focus solely on "evangelistic works," "duties" and "commitment." We run around from one meeting to another and forget the heart of Christianity, which is love and compassion for our fellow human beings. I truly believe that if we develop the heart to care for the poor and needy, we will channel that same compassion toward the lost. Jesus was powerful and intense, but he was driven by a desire to serve. Let us be like him and not get sidetracked by desires for worldly glory or position through our serving.

Think about it. Do you view helping the poor as one of the "duties" the church performs (like "Corban" in Mark 7) in which you might take part occasionally? Or do you view it as a personal responsibility to be fulfilled on a daily basis as part of being a disciple? Just as prayer, evangelism and being part of the body of Christ are essential to being a disciple, so is helping the poor (see also Matthew 6:1-4). Dorcas had truly captured the heart of her Savior.

As we read Acts 9, it is also obvious that in order to meet others' needs, Dorcas worked very hard. The people would say she had hands that heal.

Hands That Heal

We don't know if Dorcas was married or not. But if she was not a mother or grandmother to those of her bloodline, we can know that she was both to many others. We can know she made clothes for many children in her life. We don't know whether she held a secular job or not, but one thing is sure—she was a busy woman. From morning till night she would take care of others' physical needs while keeping her own household going. She was also a disciple, and so she would daily pray, focus on Jesus' teachings and share her faith. She would also meet with other Christians to pray and study together. And still she found the time to sew and do good! She was a truly amazing woman! Just like the Proverbs 31 woman, she did not "eat the bread of idleness." In those days, women did not enjoy the modern appliances we have today in the western world: dishwashers, washing machines, clothes dryers, stoves and ovens, refrigerators and vacuum cleaners. They did not have running water, electricity or cars. Work in those days was sweaty, muscle-aching, hard work!

Dorcas' schedule was full. It says in Acts 9:36 that she "was always doing good." In fact, she might have worked so hard that she got sick and died. We sometimes grumble about how busy we are. Yet how would our lives compare to hers?

Her labor also produced fruit—the disciples were able to show Peter the robes and other clothing she had made with her own hands. Could disciples use the fruit of our work as a witness to our labor and love? Could our home, our appearance, our cooking and our children testify to how early we get up and how late we go to bed? Or are our lives in disarray, causing us to be ashamed and guilt-ridden? Women disciples need to be pacesetters in the area of hard work. Sloppiness, laziness and disorganization are not Christ-like qualities. Our lives, just like Dorcas', should be upheld as examples to the world of how much we can accomplish through the power of God.

Dorcas' life was indeed an example. And so she inspired a love that is real.

When Dorcas died, crowds gathered. But these were not just the professional mourners who usually attended funerals in those days. These were genuine, sincere people who were heartbroken at her sudden death. They would miss her so much. She was deeply loved and respected because she had given so much love to so many. Dorcas was not a lonely woman—her home must have been full of people all the time. People would come and go, enjoying her hospitality and warmth. So when she passed away, they all felt bereft and bewildered, and maybe a bit displaced.

We can see how urgently they sent for Peter, who was in Lydda at the time. They were willing to travel all the way to Lydda in the distant hope that perhaps the apostle could do something. It is really amazing to realize that they were so destroyed by her death that they wouldn't accept it. Instead, they ran to Peter, probably hoping he could bring her back to life.

Disciples usually are very accepting in the face of death, knowing the person will go to be with God. But in the case of Dorcas, she was so precious and valuable to the church that they felt they couldn't do without her. How convicting! If we died, would the Christians feel that way about us? Are our lives such incredible examples of love and service that people would feel they could hardly go on without us? How much would our presence be missed?

Dorcas had a reputation as a disciple. She was outstanding in her strengths—her servanthood, her relationships, her devotion to others. People would praise her and appreciate her; the kingdom needed her. Without her, the church wasn't going to be the same, and no one could quite take her place. And that's why the Christians' faith was stretched to the point of bringing Peter over, and hoping to see her raised from the dead. May our lives also have that kind of impact today!

Dorcas Lives

The needs of people stare me in the face every day. I have spent the last seven years of my life in India. When I became a Christian, I was hardhearted and I had difficulty feeling others' pain. As a disciple, I learned that it was absolutely necessary for me to empathize with people's physical, emotional and spiritual suffering. Of course, our mission as Christians is not simply to alleviate physical pain. Yet if we learn to care at the physical level, it will soften our hearts and teach us to care at the spiritual level. Then we will truly fulfill our purpose of seeking and saving the lost.

There are probably very few places in the world where suffering is more prevalent and evident than in India. Everywhere there are people in need: people without clothes or shoes, children whose tiny little bodies are racked by disease and malnutrition, housewives trying to make do without water, electricity or money. Words cannot describe the despair and hurt in their eyes. The hearts of the disciples in the churches in India go out to them, and there are many *Dorcases* in our fellowship.

Shanthi got married at the age of 13; she is now 34 years old and has been a disciple for almost two years. She has a reputation in the church in New Delhi for always doing good and helping the poor. She is known for her hospitality: always entertaining the brothers and sisters, feeding them and giving them shelter. And yet Shanthi is poor herself. She works long hours of hard labor as a servant for a government official. She has to support her family of five, as her husband, who is not a disciple, does not feel the burden to take care of them. She makes about $50 (U.S.) per month, and yet, she is so generous. She has opened her tiny one room house to the Christians, and a family group meets there. Shanthi has a life filled with problems, but she constantly, joyfully gives to others. She can't read or write, but she gets other disciples to write for her so she can send encouraging notes to Christians. Most of the church's 350 members have been to her house for a meal at one time or another. Shanthi has the reputation of being a *Dorcas* among the disciples in New Delhi.

Not surprisingly, Shanthi is one of the most fruitful Christians in our church. One of her children is a Christian, and four of her other relatives have been converted, too. She regularly brings others to the church, many of whom have become disciples. Her life is a joy and an inspiration to all of us.

When I think of Shanthi, I get so convicted. A lot of us live comfortable lives. We have so much to give, and yet, we complain. We are selfish and complacent. We are so blind to the needs around us. As I spend more time in India, I find my heart getting softer.

Outreach to the needy has become part of my daily life. Ten years ago, I could have walked past a beggar without feeling his pain. Now, I cry often at the plight of people in need. I try to put myself in their place, to feel what they feel, and to understand them. It helps me to grow in my compassion and to be like Jesus, who was moved by the needs of the crowds (Mark 6:34).

God commands us to meet the physical needs of people. His expectation for us as Christian women is to be like Dorcas (see also 1 Timothy 5:9-10). We have a special role to fill in nurturing the disciples and reaching out to the lost. God has given women the gift of compassion. Let's cultivate that gift and not harden our hearts toward it. Let us, like Dorcas, make a difference in others' lives—for now and for eternity.

Nadine Templer
London, UK

 Is your faith "pure religion" (James 1:27) or simply a commitment to the "duties" of a disciple? Is your heart full of compassion, or is it a struggle to put yourself in others' shoes and reach out to them?

application questions on page 181

22

LYDIA
Bought for Eternity

Acts 16:11-15

Being the man chosen by God to preach the good news to the Gentiles, Paul made three missionary trips into what is now Turkey, Syria and eastern Europe. During his second sojourn, he received a vision of a man from Macedonia begging him to come help them (Acts 16:6-10). Concluding that God was directing him, he and his companions left at once. Arriving in Philippi, a Roman colony and strategic city for commerce *and* for evangelism, Paul began to preach the message of Jesus. As converts were made, they joined Paul in working for the spread of the gospel. In Macedonia women played leading roles in both the social and commercial arenas—starkly differing from the Grecian practice at the time. As in Thessalonica, another Macedonian city Paul visited, prominent women responded to the gospel and gave of their hearts and means to establish and strengthen the infant church.

◆

She who sold to royalty, became the child of *the* King. Lydia was a dynamic, hard-working woman with a heart devoted to pleasing God. God wisely chose Lydia to have the distinction and honor of being the first European convert! A "unique" woman in the community, most sources infer that Lydia must have been a widow who, for the well-being of her family, chose to carry on her husband's business. Against the odds, she had moved her family from her native Thyatira to the thriving Roman colony of Philippi. At a time when women were considered inferior and had few rights, Lydia became a successful businesswoman, surprisingly able to compete in a male-dominated economic system. How many heads must have turned in admiration as this wise, courageous woman ably marketed the rich purple fabric used for only the most regal garments and reserved for an elite segment of the society.

The testimony to her resourcefulness and consistent labor was the spacious home in which she and the members of her household must have enjoyed many hours of love and spiritual encouragement after her conversion. But what was most unique about Lydia was her heart for God. It is no wonder God's Spirit led Paul to change his travel plans and present the gospel to the future base of the great church of Philippi!

A Seeking Heart

Lydia's heart to seek after the one and only true God was evident long before that special Sabbath day when she accepted Jesus and was baptized. She had the heart to renounce the religion of the majority—the religion with which she was raised. She decided against "worshipping" with a large established pagan assembly within the city limits, where her pool of potential clients would be larger and her time commitment would be smaller. Lydia thought first of how she could grow in the love and knowledge of her God, trusting that he would richly bless her family and business.

God responded to Lydia's heart in ways that neither she nor Paul had expected. We read in Acts 16:13 that on the Sabbath, Paul and his companions were looking for a place of prayer. Lydia, the *Godfearer,* and a small group of Jewish women were joined together to worship God. Then both groups met. Paul could have thought, *I was kept from advancing the kingdom in the province of Asia to evangelize a few Jewish WOMEN?!* Little did Paul know that he was on the verge of proclaiming the gospel to a woman who would surrender her wealth, her home and her very being to plant what would become one of the churches most dear to his heart.

Lydia is known for her responsiveness to the gospel. In fact, her name has become synonymous with a woman eager to study God's Word. Acts 16:14 says, "The Lord opened [Lydia's] heart to respond to Paul's message." As a result, she was baptized, along with the members of her household. We do not know exactly who the members of her household were—servants and/or family—but evidently they trusted enough in Lydia's spiritual discernment to follow her lead. We read nothing about hesitation or consideration of what people would think about her "joining this new religion." All we see is an unfettered zeal to be united with her Father.

A Serving Heart

When we think of Lydia, we think of hospitality. Her gratitude for her newly-found salvation and purpose compelled her to "persuade" Paul and his companions to stay at her house. It is not hard to picture Lydia saying, "No, I insist!" Isn't it refreshing to see such a spontaneous outpouring of love? Nobody had to coax her or ask for volunteers. Who knows how many Christians experienced the warmth of her home? Who knows how many meals she served or how many needs she met? Paul had been an example to her of not serving in order to be repaid or praised. She understood right from the start that it was an honor and privilege to serve the Lord's messengers.

A Confident Heart

Though Lydia is known for her seeking and her serving, she must also be remembered for her godly confidence. She came into the kingdom with a great deal of worldly confidence. But it was her trust in God, not in her wealth or position of influence, which allowed her to be a spiritual leader among the disciples at Philippi. For example, when Paul and Silas escaped from prison, Lydia welcomed them into her home, possibly risking her business and her own personal safety. And even though she had just been baptized and had no "position" in the church, she was not intimidated by Paul. "If you consider me a believer in the Lord," she said, "come stay at my house." Luke adds, "And she persuaded us" (Acts 16:15).

Lydia was wise, and practical enough, to realize that she could learn much from Paul, but she also had enough confidence in herself to insist on being Paul's hostess. She did not minimize herself or avoid responsibility in a falsely humble way, but rather, sincerely believed that she could have an impact on Christians and non-Christians alike. You can say she was a bit audacious, but it seems more true to say that she was not afraid to acknowledge her many God-given talents. In fact, Lydia was probably quite proud that her home was the nucleus of the Philippian church, and she likely was not surprised that the first place Paul and Silas would go upon escaping from prison would be her house!

It is easy to perceive Lydia's influence on the Philippian disciples. "I thank my God every time I remember you. In all my prayers for all of you, I always pray with joy because of your partnership in the gospel from the first day until now..." (Philippians 1:3-5). These were the words Paul penned just a few years after that history-making Sabbath. Tears must have clouded Lydia's eyes as she read Paul's letter, or heard it read, and affectionately remembered the meals they had shared together, the wounds she had nursed, and the prayers they had offered up to God along with the church.

Although Paul's words were written to the entire church, they can't help but remind us of Lydia. After all, she had been there "from the first day." The heart of this exemplary disciple still speaks today through the pages of Philippians. We must never forget how much one day can change our lives nor how much one woman can change multitudes for eternity.

Obstacles As Opportunities

Lydia, though extremely talented, was an unlikely candidate to be such an incredible person of impact. First, she was a woman, not to mention a widow and possibly even a single mother, living in the midst of intense persecution. Yet she did not focus on obstacles. It doesn't even seem as if she thought there *were* obstacles!

Unlike Lydia, my sinful nature is to be negative and think of why something *can't* be done rather than how it *can* be done. Or even if I don't let the obstacles deter me from my ultimate goal, I tend to let them steal my joy. Sometimes I catch myself whining (ugh!). The ultimate in being convicted , though, is when my husband, John, tells me I need to "put on a happy face." What I need to imitate in Lydia is her positive outlook (otherwise known as faith!). I need to look at *obstacles* as *opportunities* to grow in my faith and dependence on God. Last year, God gave me the situation I needed to enable me to change a great deal in this area. Both my son and daughter, ages four and two, respectively, had very serious health problems. I can't begin to count the hours I spent in hospitals, doctor's offices and laboratories. I can't accurately describe the constant pit in my stomach as I watched my children undergo test after test. At the same time, my husband and I assumed the leadership of a new church and increased responsibilities. I knew Satan wanted me to fold under the pressure. I vividly remember the day we received some particularly bad news from the doctor. The first thing we did was pull over to the side of the road to pray. We told God we would trust him. We told him we would not lose our focus. And we asked him to help us baptize a couple with a child who had problems similar to those of our son.

Thanks be to God, both of my children's health has miraculously improved. We have had victories in our ministries. Less than a year after we prayed that prayer, God blessed us with a couple from our son's school becoming disciples. Yet, I consider the true victory to be my having looked beyond the obstacles to see the Almighty God.

I hate that I still have to fight "tooth and nail" against my negative nature. I know it is so wrong not to trust God when he has proven his love for me in such a powerful way through Jesus. I know, however, that I have much hope of change because Lydia was an overcomer! Let us overwhelmingly embrace her inspiring example.

Barbara Porter
Miami, USA

 FOCUS   Do you tend to see difficult situations as obstacles or as opportunities? What can help you keep a godly perspective in hard times?

application questions on page 181

23

PRISCILLA
Sold Out, Not Burned Out

---

*Acts 18:1-4, 18-28; Romans 16:3; 1 Corinthians 16:19;
2 Timothy 4:19*

Jews are no strangers to persecution. During the first century, Claudius, Emperor of Rome (A.D. 41-54), ordered all Jews to leave Rome—simply to turn their backs on their homes, their jobs, their synagogues and to leave. The reason? "Their continual tumults instigated by Christus." If Christus refers to Christ, which in all likelihood it does, the unrest and riots would have been *because* of him, not by him.

Some of these displaced people were natives of other regions, but for some Rome had always been home. Nevertheless, they were Jews, and they were a bother. A husband and wife obeyed and sailed for Corinth. They were expelled by the hand of an Emperor only to be blessed by the hand of God.

◆

Exiled! Satan and the world screamed, *"Get out; we hate you, your God and your faith!"* It was one of those times when life is at its toughest. A time when some women are tempted to give up, blame God and their husbands, and simply burn out spiritually. Priscilla, a Pontus Jewess, along with her husband Aquila, withstood the test and remained faithful to her God and to her husband. She was truly a woman after God's own heart, thereby becoming one of the most, if not *the* most, influential women in the first-century church.

In the six references to her in the New Testament, she is always mentioned along with her husband. These two hearts beat as one as they labored together in the service of the Lord and his kingdom. Three of those times she is mentioned first, possibly denoting her strength of character and impact. Also, some sources indicate that Priscilla may have come from a well-to-do, influential family. One other possibility is that she had become a Christian first and had won her husband to Christ by her submissive spirit and pure life (1 Peter 3:1-2).

Get Out!

When she first heard the news, she shook her head in disbelief. She took a deep breath and slowly let it out as she looked around her at the house they had furnished and decorated. She knew that all of these things did not hold her life; her God held her life. But she did hold all these things, and now she must part with most, if not all, of them. Her crime? Being a Jew. She had hurt no one, broken no law, given no reason for banishment other than her birth.

As they closed the door behind them with a solid, no-turning-back thud, she exchanged glances with other Jewish friends who were walking past. They did not need to say anything; their eyes and their stooping shoulders said it all.

A New Life

Priscilla and Aquila began their new lives in Corinth in 49 A.D. where shortly thereafter they met and teamed up with the apostle Paul. We don't know for sure whether they became Christians in Rome, or if they were converted by Paul after they met him. Whichever the case, not only did they become partners in the tentmaking business, but they became powerful partners in the Gospel.

What a blessing to have Paul in their home! To get up in the morning and have breakfast with him as he started his day. To see the earnestness with which he prayed to God and planned the evangelization of not only Corinth, but all of the known world. To learn how to respond to persecution, how to challenge the Jews to faith in Jesus, how to encourage the disciples. This was discipling at its purest and best.

Paul had not entered Corinth with great confidence in himself. In fact, he admits that he came to the city "in weakness and fear, and with much trembling" (1 Corinthians 2:3). By all worldly appearances, he did not look like a powerful leader who was going to turn a city upside down. What a joy and encouragement it must have been for Paul to stay in the home of a couple who would support him and share his burning passion for the mission. Along with such Christians as Crispus, Gais and Stephanas' household, this couple formed the nucleus of the church in Corinth (1 Corinthians 1:13-16). Seeing and being a part of these first conversions gave Priscilla and Aquila great vision for what God could accomplish in their city and region. They must have been thrilled to see many more Corinthians who heard, believed, were baptized, and then took their faith in Christ deeper.

Making Disciples Together

Paul raised up this exemplary couple in the Lord, who not only were co-workers in business and partners in the gospel, but also best friends. They accompanied Paul to Cenchrea in anticipation of sailing with him to Syria. While they were in Cenchrea, Paul got his hair cut as part of a vow he had taken (Acts 18:18-19). Quite possibly, while Priscilla was in that seacoast town, she was able to spend time with another friend of Paul—the mature and trustworthy Phoebe. These two women would have been great "sharpeners" for each other's faith and character. They were strong women who had given their hearts to God and his kingdom.

After sailing to Ephesus, Paul went on to Antioch to visit the churches and strengthen the disciples. Priscilla and Aquila stayed for a time, possibly opening a branch of their business there. It was during this time that Apollos, an Alexandrian Jew, arrived in Ephesus. He had been baptized after the manner of John the Baptist, but had not experienced the gift of the Holy Spirit. This eloquent, learned man argued powerfully about Jesus in the synagogue. Priscilla and Aquila heard him and invited him into their home where they explained the way of God more adequately (Acts 18:26).

This is one of the passages in which Priscilla's name is mentioned first. If she did indeed have a higher social standing than Aquila, she may have been better educated and more able to communicate with the learned Apollos. Priscilla must have learned to turn her talents over to God to bring glory to him and not to herself. Because of their continuing unity, we must infer that Aquila was supportive of his wife and not easily threatened by her gifts.

A Hospitable Heart

Priscilla's hospitable heart is worthy of imitation. In Corinth she and her husband had quickly invited Paul to stay with them. Then in Ephesus, they again quickly invited Apollos to their home. No superficial convert herself, she was determined that this eminent man should be well-informed so as to powerfully advance God's kingdom.

A determined woman, Priscilla was ready to do what was needed on the spot. She was truly willing to do anything, go anywhere, change anything at any time for the sake of God's kingdom. Her whole life was characterized by the "whatever-it-takes-to-do-your-will-and-advance-your-kingdom,-I-will-do-it" attitude. Sounds like Jesus, doesn't it? No sacrifice was too great, not too many people on her carpet or too many meetings in her home getting it dirty. Priscilla's house was God's house because her heart was God's home.

Later Paul wrote his first letter to the Corinthians from Ephesus and sent warm greetings from Aquila and "Prisca" and the church meeting at their house (1 Corinthians 16:19). In those early days of the church, poverty and persecution made separate buildings for worship impractical, so private homes were used as the gathering places for the saints. No doubt Priscilla and Aquila had a passionate desire to unite God's people in fellowship as they used their home for the Lord in this way.

A Matter of Life and Death

No one could spend time with Paul and miss the fact that becoming a disciple was a matter of life and death. Whether Priscilla and Aquila were involved in the silversmith riots in Ephesus or in some danger there, it is not known. We do know that they, at some point, risked their lives for Paul, earning the heartfelt gratitude of all the Gentile churches (Romans 16:3-4). They saved the man the Lord had consecrated to the service of the Gentile world.

Following the death of the Emperor Claudius, the edict of banishment was no longer enforced. It is possible that Priscilla and Aquila returned to Rome, retaining their business in Ephesus, and traveled freely between the two cities.

Tradition has it that they ultimately laid down their lives for Christ's sake, being led out beyond the walls and beheaded in Rome. Priscilla's exemplary faith, devotion to God and her husband and her love for people had a profound impact on the first-century church. Even though she was not on the "church payroll," she gave one hundred percent to her Lord and Savior. She never *held back or burned out*. She used every talent and resource to the glory of God. Like her Savior, she did everything well—a woman sold out for God who remained sold out to the very end.

Just Do It!

As I've read, studied and prayed about Priscilla, I have been inspired by her heart for God, for her husband, for the church and the lost. She is a woman who could have taken life easy and done a few good things for people to salve her conscience. Instead, she poured out her money, time and energy for God and others. I praise God for giving us her example to follow.

Like Priscilla, I must walk closely with God daily if I am to be sold out and victorious for God and his kingdom. I realize more than ever that without Jesus, I can do nothing! When my love for Christ and his people has been weak, my life has shown the weakness. When my times with God have been weak, shallow, rushed and cut short, my life has shown it and has become ugly. I am learning to stop making excuses for my lack of a growing heart for God. I've got to respond as the popular slogan says, "Just Do It." *Do it* because I am so grateful and love God so much. I have to get humble, get open and get help! I've got to take it deeper all the time.

I'm so thankful to God for prayer times, prayer walks and quiet times with my husband, Martin, and with my sisters in the kingdom. Through open and honest times with committed disciples, I've been able to draw closer to God's heart.

I was also inspired by Priscilla's marriage. She was completely united in spirit and purpose with Aquila her husband. Encouraging and following his lead, she was his helpmate in advancing the kingdom of God, building up the saints as they opened their home to all, and reaching out to the lost together. Recently, I discovered that the scriptures about love, submission, humility, serving and unity were in my head, but they weren't in my heart. Again, this showed up in my life. I spent more energy being prideful, making excuses, not following closely, doing things *my way* and not the way Martin had asked me to do them. I had more criticism than support in my heart, and I blamed him all the while for our lack of closeness and impact. Discipling, great examples and repentance are sweet—and refreshing, too! I'm thankful for Kip and Elena McKean (my sister) who have loved me, challenged me and whom God has used to help me to change in these areas. I'm thankful for great examples, sisters and disciplers that God has put in my life to show me the way to love, to be submissive to, and to be a united teammate with my incredible and merciful husband. I had to come to the realization that until my marriage was godly, God couldn't use me to my greatest potential to help others.

Satan will always try to hold us back. We've got to look at the woman in the mirror and repent. Then the Lord will use us with our families, the saints and the lost in a powerful way to his glory, as he did Priscilla.

Carmen Garcia Bentley
San Diego, USA

 FOCUS   What do you need to change in your relationship with God, with your husband, with brothers and sisters in the kingdom and with the lost to be completely sold out for God?

application questions on page 182

24
DRUSILLA AND BERNICE
Twisted Sisters

Acts 23:26-24:27; 25:13-26:32

In Drusilla and Bernice we find even more rotten fruit from the family tree of the Herods. Their grandfather, Herod Antipas, was the one who beheaded John the Baptist, and their father, Herod Agrippa I, had carried on the family tradition by beheading the apostle James.

By their association with Paul, these two women could have understood the unfolding plan of God. The Jesus who Paul preached was the one who their great-grandfather had tried to kill. At the time, though, he had been safe in Egypt, far from the godless slaughter in Galilee. He was protected by the Father who loved him and who loved us all. And now this Jesus had died for the sins of the whole world, even the family of Herod. They could have come to know him, and they could have broken the chain of sin and evil that had infested the Herods for so many generations. They could have, but in their arrogance, they didn't.

◆

Drusilla and Bernice would be great principal characters for a first-century television miniseries. Sex. Power. Prestige. Incest. Politics. They are all there—in abundance. Sisters, by blood and by wickedness, they showed why their people long before spoke a certain proverb, "The fathers eat sour grapes, and the children's teeth are set on edge" (Ezekiel 18: 2). *We cannot help being bad. Look at our heritage.* Although God abhorred the sentiment of this proverb, surely Bernice and Drusilla would have accepted its message and excused themselves from any responsibility for their godless lives. There is no question that their Herodian bloodline both *ate,* and forced upon others, *many bunches* of sour grapes.

Pernicious Pedigree

Drusilla and Bernice were born in A.D. 38 and 28 respectively. Their great-grandfather, Herod the Great, was so threatened by the prophecies of Christ's birth that he committed the atrocity of slaughtering innocent babies in his zeal to kill the coming Messiah (Matthew 2:16). Their grandfather was Herod Antipas whose lust for Salome, and incautious promise to her, led him to authorize the murder of John the Baptist (Matthew 14:6-11). Their father was Herod Agrippa I, first systematic persecutor of the church (Acts 12:1-4). Pride, among other sins, doubtless brought his life to a terrible end (Acts 12:23). Their brother was Agrippa II, tetrarch, and later, king. There is no evidence to the contrary that these women escaped the moral corruption inherent in their ancestry.

Growing up in this family, their role models were men of great standing and notoriety who could have used their power to effect great changes for good in society. They instead used their position to gain for themselves whatever their sinful nature craved, indulging in whichever lust or vanity took their fancy.

Scandalous Sisters

The notoriety of these two women is evident in several extra-biblical accounts of first century history. In *The Histories* by Tacitus and *The Jewish War* and *Antiquities* by Josephus, they are mentioned unfavorably. Perhaps the most revealing insight into Bernice is her appearance in *Satire VI* by Juvenal which, in one passage, cites a ring given to her by her brother Agrippa II "as a token of their incestuous love."[1]

Character is formed at such a young age, and undoubtedly, family members play the key role. As Proverbs 22:6 says, "Train up a child in the way he should go, and when he is old he will not turn from it." Family affects us for good—or for bad. As young girls, Drusilla and Bernice would have grown up hearing stories about the way their forefathers had dealt with any godly influence which threatened their position, power and comfort. How hard it would have been to grow up with a father who was so arrogant and egotistical that God had him struck down by an angel and eaten by worms (Acts 12:23).

What kind of trust could there be of a father who would compromise any values to maintain the praise of people, but cared nothing for the praise of God? What security could exist when even your own brother looked at you lustfully? Then, tradition has it that

---

[1] Line 1, 156-160

Bernice was envious of younger sister Drusilla's beauty and, consequently, treated her very badly. Imagine the taunting and cruelty that would be endured, the tensions at the dinner table. Many of us have either *had* a bossy big sister or we have *been* one. Can you imagine having a bossy big sister in the Herodian family?

Knowing human nature, we can imagine that their inward struggles of bitterness and envy would surely have led them to an ever-increasing game of one-upmanship. Who could attract the most admirers? Who could find the most expensive and beautiful garments? Who could be the most outrageous? By the dictates of an uncurbed sinful nature, each would have been *aggressively* looking out for herself and her own interests, not the interests of the other.

It is sad that for all their privileges, their money and power, they were only driven to greater bitterness and isolation from each other—and to greater emptiness.

Rotten Relationships

You can tell much about a woman by considering the nature of her relationships. Revealing insights into both of our women can be found by looking at their list of male companions. According to Josephus, Drusilla was given by her father in marriage to the Syrian king Azizus (probably a politically motivated union). Later she was persuaded by Felix to leave Azizus and marry him instead! He reportedly promised her "that if she would not refuse him, he would make her a happy woman."[2] Felix, governor of Judea, had a reputation for brutality, power-lust and corruption. It was he who reputedly ended the terrorist revolt mentioned in Acts 21:38. Clearly, he was familiar with the religious and political movements of his day and would generally commit any act of cruelty to quash them. Drusilla married this man.

Bernice, at the age of 13, married her uncle, Herod of Chalcis. By all accounts, after his death, she engaged in an incestuous relationship with her brother, Agrippa II. Subsequently, she married Polemon, king of Cilicia, deserted him for her brother and later became the mistress of Titus, the future Emperor.

The lifestyles of these rich and famous people were characterized by an empty amorality. Their desire to be happy led them to seek

[2] Josephus 20, 7, 2

more and more indulgence in the sensual pleasures of life. The more they *ate*, the more *sick* they became. Like their forefathers, they became women who were prepared to compromise any values to go where their selfishness and vanity led them.

The Apostle's Audience

Paul had been arrested in Jerusalem, appeared before the Sanhedrin and, because a conspiracy against him was uncovered, he was transported to Caesarea to be tried by Felix (Acts 23:23-24). Felix, seemingly politically sensitive to the Jews (Acts 24:2, 27), called upon Paul to explain himself. Felix and Drusilla heard the message of Christ from the apostle's lips. Interestingly enough, the only recorded response is that Felix was afraid and terminated the discourse. Afraid of what? That he might be persuaded? Afraid of whom? A man with such courage and boldness, or God himself? Drusilla's only mention in the Bible—her chance to hear, repent and obey the gospel—records no response. A Jewess, obviously religiously and politically aware, she must have had a harder heart than her famously vicious Roman husband, who at least understood enough to be afraid.

Bernice and Agrippa arrived in Caesarea to greet Felix's successor Festus (Acts 25:13). A valuable insight into Bernice's style is gained in Acts 25:23. She was consorting with high-ranking officers and the city's leading men in an atmosphere of pomp and ceremony. Would the prospect of witnessing to the gospel before such a brazen woman and her incestuous brother/lover deter Paul from preaching an uncompromising message? As we read in Acts 26, Paul clearly appealed to this branch of the Herodian family, assuring them that Satan's hold on their lives could be broken by faith and repentance. Again, interestingly enough, it was the man who showed a response. Agrippa responded to Paul's question with his own obviously insecure question as he felt the inevitability of the gospel's truth: "Do you think that in such a short time you can persuade me to be a Christian?" (Acts 26:28). No response is recorded from Bernice— except the implication of indifference (Acts 26:31). Unaware of her own spiritual plight, she dismissed the apostle's message. After Paul is sent to Rome, we read nothing further of Drusilla or Bernice.

Paul walked out of these two women's lives, and they locked the already closed door to their hearts.

Hesitant or Heroic?

I am challenged by Paul's incredible zeal to preach the Word in any and every situation! God had chosen him to preach before kings (Acts 9:15) and he never hesitated to obey God's destiny for him.

As I studied these passages, I became increasingly convicted by Paul's attitude. If I encounter a group of impressive women, my first response has not been to imitate Paul boldly and impact these women on the spot. Rather, my thoughts have been focused on my own weaknesses and their perception of me. Even though Paul was brought before them on trial, he did not present himself as a victim. Rather, he clearly portrayed himself as a victor—along with his crucified and risen Lord! Even in such a challenging situation among high-powered people, he was assured of his purpose. I must imitate his heart and his courage if I am to impact prominent women.

Jesus, with all authority, commands me to go and make disciples of all the world (Matthew 28:18-20). In essence, is my charge any different from Paul's as the apostle to the Gentiles? This study has challenged me to carry out this charge—to preach to people of great prominence. Drusilla and Bernice certainly needed God, though they remained hard-hearted to Paul's message. I must see people in the same way Paul did!

One thing I need to remember is that many prominent women *did* respond to the gospel in the New Testament. I must envision people as Paul did, for he never hesitated to obey God and preach the truth. Some, like Drusilla and Bernice, will remain worldly and indifferent, but others will be open to the gospel. As we die to ourselves, obey God and imitate Paul's courage, we will see more and more women like this converted!

Emma Scott
London, UK

FOCUS

When you are in the company of prominent, impressive women, are you secure in your faith? Do you speak your heart and your mind?

application questions on page 182

25

WEAK-WILLED WOMEN
Always Learning, Never Knowing

2 Timothy 3:6-7

The church in Ephesus had to hold a special place in Paul's heart. His son in the faith, Timothy, was the evangelist, and his good friends, Priscilla and Aquila, were Timothy's coworkers. As he wrote the letter we know as Second Timothy, Paul was in a damp Roman jail—held captive by Nero. He suffered "even to the point of being chained like a criminal" (2 Timothy 2:9). His concern for the Ephesian church was, no doubt, heightened by his impending death. He issued warnings about false teachers and eventual apostasy. His charge to Timothy must have been written with tears and deep conviction: "Preach the Word; be prepared in season and out of season; correct, rebuke and encourage—with great patience and careful instruction" (2 Timothy 4:2). One of his concerns had to do with teachers who had "a form of godliness" but denied its real power (2 Timothy 3:5).

◆

They are the kind who worm their way into homes and gain control over weak-willed women, who are loaded down with sins and are swayed by all kinds of evil desires, always learning but never able to acknowledge the truth (2 Timothy 3:6-7).

She strolled leisurely through the dusty streets, her eyes wandering from side to side to take in the sights. The market was crowded, full of people selling, buying and bargaining. Fish was being sold from the waters of the Aegean Sea. Fruits, freshly shipped in from nearby Achaia, yielded a sweet aroma, enticing anyone who walked past. Bread, oil and vegetables were traded for shiny coins. She made her transactions without much thought...her mind was elsewhere. The attractive woman was thinking of the intriguing man she heard speak the night before near the temple of Artemis. She had been learning so much lately!

First, the itinerant preacher Paul had come to teach about the great rabbi, Jesus, who had been cruelly killed but had been raised from the dead. Paul had claimed that all believers could participate in life after death if they followed this Jesus. Paul's young friend Timothy was constantly preaching to the Ephesians about Jesus, and she had learned much from him. Later, the handsome Philetus had proclaimed that no one could really be raised from the dead physically, but that everyone could participate in a spiritual, symbolic "resurrection." Then Micah preached so fervently about the hidden knowledge that only angels knew, and had told so many fascinating tales that opened up new worlds of thought to her. And now Luxor had sailed across the Mediterranean Sea from Egypt to Ephesus to proclaim more deep truths about religion...he seemed so spiritual, so "godlike" to her. Surely he could help her learn even more!

What did it matter that some of the preachers contradicted one another? She could simply take from each teaching the things that felt right to her and leave behind the rest. What really mattered was that she was improving her mind, becoming more of a deep thinker. Surely all these new thoughts would bring about the fulfillment she longed for!

As she walked past the stalls of the market, she spied the lush, magnificent grapes she loved so much. Too expensive! But the vendor was busy with another customer...surely he wouldn't notice just one bunch missing. She remembered that Paul had taught that Jesus wouldn't want his followers to steal, but didn't Luxor just say last night that life was too fleeting to worry oneself with little flaws in character? Quickly she shuffled the grapes into her bag and walked on. No one saw!

She noticed a woman selling incense and shouting out, "These aromas will call back the dead!" She ignored the woman. She had spent many coins on things like this, and none of them worked. Her disappointment had been acute, and she had vowed that she would only go to reputable mediums in the future.

As she stepped past a gathering of soldiers, her walk took on a new sway. The men noticed her, and she felt the thrill of their stares. Although she had always been faithful to her husband, certainly there was nothing wrong with thinking about other men. She brushed aside the vague remembrance of something she heard about Jesus.

Had he said it was wrong to think lustfully? Oh no, he could not have meant that. Surely there is no harm in it!

She sighed as she headed toward her house, bracing herself for the tasks of the day. It was early, and already she was weary. She felt burdened by the work she knew she must do to help in her family's business, in addition to caring for her family and her home. She remembered bickering with her husband that morning, and dreaded facing him. She felt a nagging guilt as the weight of the grapes in the bag grew heavy. Boredom and discontent were all that welcomed her into the house; her family was away for the day. She began her work, not noticing the sound of the footsteps that were approaching. The knock startled her. Who could be coming to visit her? Opening the door, she was surprised and pleased to see Luxor, the eloquent teacher she had listened to last night. He stood in the doorway, tall and smiling. "I understand you are interested in my teachings," he said softly. "May I come in, so that we may talk more?" She opened her door wide to the man, looking forward to learning all about Luxor's religion—and all about Luxor.

Convictions Without Sway

We considered ourselves so fortunate. We were teenagers in the 1960s and '70s, and we didn't have to conform to traditional values or lifestyles. We had new ideas, new thinking, and we didn't have to settle for the status quo of the older generation. We were revolutionaries...and we had it all. We were seekers. We were learners.

But where did all our new ideas and education get us? Free sex, drugs and the hippie movement proved to be empty and unfulfilling. For myself, the more I learned, the more desolate I became. I scoffed at religion and held the philosophy of the song, "I'll swear there ain't no heaven, and I'll pray there ain't no hell." Like the weak-willed women that Paul wrote about, I was always learning but never able to acknowledge the truth. Thanks to some true "revolutionaries" in my life, I was able to find the truth about Jesus and become his disciple. I was able to learn the truth from the Bible, to know it, and to live it. God planted his truth in my heart, and it is still rooted there, bringing me confidence and blessings.

We, as Christian women, are not immune to the dangers of becoming weak-willed. Often we are sentimental and don't want to draw the lines that God draws. We think it's "strong" to be independent and do things our own way, when often that way is the easiest of all. We make decisions or follow philosophies that are from the world and not from God. Ultimately, we think we know better than God. Truths that we once held dear become vague and difficult. We lose our convictions! *Convictions* are what keep us grounded in the truth. *Convictions* are what free us from the burdens of sin. *Convictions* are what keep us from being swayed by our own evil desires.

My temptations are the same as most any woman's. I want people to like me. I want to be considered attractive. I want to be comfortable. I want it easy. I don't want conflict. I could easily give in to any of these temptations on any given day. This is what I use to fight these temptations: *my convictions.* I go back to the Bible and see what Jesus says, how Jesus lived. I pray for strength to help me through the battles. I *know* God's word is true, and I strive to live by it. I am not perfect, and I sometimes fail, but my convictions push me to get up when I fall—and to try harder next time.

I see the value of having an open mind. Unfortunately, some women's minds are so open that nothing stays in them! As disciples, we must make sure that we are always learning: *learning how to follow Christ more closely.* We must make sure our convictions don't become watered down. We must hold on tightly to the truths of God's Word, knowing that in so doing we will be blessed. I thank God that he has allowed me to know the truth, to acknowledge the truth and to live the truth. It has set me free!

Kay McKean
Boston, USA

FOCUS

Are you easily swayed by new and interesting ideas, or are you grounded firmly in convictions from the Scriptures?

application questions on page 182

26

EUODIA AND SYNTYCHE
Work It Out!

Philippians 4:2-3

From a Roman prison Paul wrote to the Philippian church with warmth and fatherly affection. His ties to this group seemed to be especially close. In several cases, his camaraderie with Christian sisters is mentioned (Acts 16:13-15). He held these women in high esteem and worked side by side with them and others to make known the riches of a relationship with God through Jesus Christ (Acts 17:4, 12).

His concerns for his spiritual children were obvious. The church was experiencing intense local persecution, possibly even mob violence. Most of the disciples were probably Gentile (a reasonable assumption since there was no synagogue in Philippi). They had given up false gods and were incurring the wrath of friends and family. In addition to the foes outside of the group, false teachers were abundant and deceptive within the group. The need for unity among disciples was paramount.

◆

I plead with Euodia and I plead with Syntyche to agree with each other in the Lord. Yes, and I ask you, loyal yokefellow, help these women who have contended at my side in the cause of the gospel, along with Clement and the rest of my fellow workers, whose names are in the book of life (Philippians 4:2-3).

We just don't get along! It's a personality clash! I do respect her; it's just that we are very different. She's just not my type. We don't know the nature of the disagreement between Euodia and Syntyche. Maybe it was doctrinal or personal, or maybe they didn't agree about how things should be done. Whatever it was, Paul needed to plead with them from his prison cell to sort out their differences.

Isn't it interesting that Paul doesn't take sides? He doesn't discuss who was right and who was wrong, or even partly right and partly wrong. He doesn't even mention the problem by name; he just urges the women to sort it out—to resolve it. He calls on their friends to help them, but emphatically his tone is, "Deal with it; settle matters quickly." Having "contended" at Paul's side, we know that these women were not young Christians. They had helped Paul when he was in Philippi. According to some sources, they were house church leaders. Euodia and Syntyche must have been aware of previous teachings by Paul on the importance of resolving conflict in the church. Surely the words of Jesus would have been uppermost in Paul's heart and mind as he taught the Philippian disciples:

> "If your brother sins against you, go and show him his fault, just between the two of you. If he listens to you, you have won your brother over. But if he will not listen, take one or two others along..." (Matthew 18:15-16).

Did these two women talk things over with each other? Did either of them initiate? Did they go to other people for help? We don't know! What we do know is that at the time of the writing, they were not righteous in their pursuit of a unified solution to their problem.

The Special Reading

Imagine Euodia and Syntyche sitting in the assembly, eagerly awaiting the reading of Paul's letter. They were great friends with Paul and had been loyal workers with him. *The elder reads Paul's greetings, and the women, who at this stage are sitting on opposite sides of the room, smile inwardly at Paul's praise of their Philippian fellowship. Then he urges everyone to have Christ's humility, to be "like-minded," to be "one in spirit and purpose"! Does Euodia feel convicted? As the elder continues to read, "Do nothing out of selfish ambition or vain conceit, but in humility consider others better than yourself," does Syntyche decide to be humble and make the first move toward being resolved?*

Maybe each is waiting for the other to take the first reconciliatory step. Suddenly, the room goes quiet and the words of Paul echo across the room. "I plead with Euodia and I plead with Syntyche to agree with each other in the Lord." Two heads held high in pride and smug self-righteousness are lowered in shame!!

Assuming Euodia was the older of the two, she should have taken responsibility to humble herself and approach her sister. Being a Christian longer should only make us more humble, not less, and more eager to *accept* responsibility, not more eager to *shift* responsibility and defend ourselves. Maturity in Christ means that we are the first to initiate when there is disunity, and we certainly are the last to cause it. Waiting for the younger Christian to come and apologize is not conducting ourselves "in a manner worthy of the gospel of Christ" (Philippians 1:27).

The Spiritual Reality

Paul's attitude towards his fellow Christians was expressed in Philippians 4:1 "...whom I love and long for, my joy and crown." Paul really loved the brothers and sisters in Philippi with a deep, emotional longing. If we felt for each other like Paul did, we would certainly recognize the evil of division and disunity. If Euodia had remembered that Christ died for Syntyche as well as herself, maybe the conflict between them would have been resolved much quicker. The kingdom needs us to be radical in our love for each other, not lukewarm.

Paul wasn't concerned so much with the disagreement itself as he was with the fact that it could cause divisions in the body. Paul wanted the other members of the church to help, to get involved. As James 4:17 says, to know the good we ought to do and not do it, is sin. To see disunity, to feel tension among Christians and yet stand aloof, is wrong. How can a kingdom advance if it fights among itself? Only a unified church, where Euodia and Syntyche are fighting together "in the cause of the gospel" (Philippians 4:3), could present a united front against the world. Paul knew that where there is disharmony within, there is bound to be defeat without. He doubtless prayed Jesus' prayer for his followers, that "all of them may be one...so that the world may believe..." (John 17:21). Paul had come to believe in the power of *one*.

Plead with Yourself

I don't think she really appreciates me. We're so different. I don't think she likes me. Thoughts from the heart of Euodia or Syntyche? No!! Thoughts from the heart of Jackie McGrath, 10 years ago. When I first started thinking about Euodia and Syntyche, I wondered how two

Christians could not get along, especially after they had been through so much together. Then I reminded myself that I behaved the same way with a roommate before I was married. Was it a deep doctrinal issue? I think not! Was she practicing a sin that she kept secret and only I knew? No! This was a much more complicated issue, one that most women are used to: FEELINGS!

I was a very young Christian, and she was very different from me. As I look back, I can now see that most of her strengths were my weaknesses. However, at the time, I felt threatened by those strengths and became very proud in my heart towards her. Thoughts like *She doesn't respect me* or *I just don't feel close to her* are a sure sign to me that my eyes are focused on myself, not on God or his kingdom. This was illustrated by the fact that the whole year I lived with her, I was not personally fruitful.

Fortunately, a "true yokefellow" in my life—Joyce Arthur—urged me to sort it out and resolve our differences. The sad thing was that I realized that many of the things I thought she said or thought she implied were complete misunderstandings on my part. I'll never forget how hurt she felt as I poured out my judgment on her. We became great friends from that day and went on to lead ministries together. Now, if I don't feel close to a sister or brother, I see it as a warning sign and am much more eager to resolve it, to agree with each other in the Lord.

The specifics of the conflict between Euodia and Syntyche are not described, but we can fill in the blank with our own details. Likewise, the "true yokefellow" is left anonymous, but here, also, we may put our own names. We should always be alert to discern and then quick to heal the cancer of division and disunity in our group, our marriage and our church.

Jackie McGrath
Washington DC, USA

 Is there unresolved conflict in your life? Look at how it is affecting your group, your ministry, your marriage. Deal with it today and, if need be, enlist a "true yokefellow" to help.

application questions on page 183

27

EUNICE AND LOIS
Faithful Forerunners

Acts 14:8-23; Acts 16:1-5; 2 Timothy 1:5; 3:14-15

A visit from Zeus and Hermes—the lead Greek god and his spokesperson. That's what the Lystrans thought was happening when Barnabas and Paul arrived during their first missionary journey. After they performed the miracle of healing a man born crippled, the people concluded that surely this was a visit from the gods. Sources indicate that an ancient legend told of a visit by the two gods. In the legend, only one poor couple welcomed them, so the whole city was punished for their lack of hospitality. Obviously, the people of Lystra did not want to make that mistake again and to suffer those consequences. After finally dissuading the people from sacrificing to them, Paul and Barnabas preached the message of Jesus for the first time in a Gentile area.

After some time, Jews from Antioch and Iconium came over to stir up trouble for them (a six- or seven-day journey by foot). They were successful in their mission and, as a result, Paul was stoned and left for dead. Whether he was resurrected or just revived is not clear, but God certainly worked miraculously to allow him to be on the road again with his companions the next morning, going to Derbe to preach. Among the people who responded to the message and became disciples in Lystra were Eunice, a Jewess with a heart for God, and, in all likelihood, her mother Lois as well.

◆

The time had come—the time for which she had spent years preparing—the time for Timothy to leave home. She, as well as her mother, Lois, and her teenage son, Timothy, eagerly anticipated Paul's return to Lystra after several years of waiting. Yet, she was unprepared for Paul's request that Timothy accompany him on his travels. She was familiar with Paul's travels—how vividly she remembered his first time in Lystra. It was a time that changed not only her life but also that of her mother and son for eternity! As she strained her eyes to get one last glimpse of Paul and her young Timothy before the road curved out of sight, tears welled up, her throat tightened, but her heart was full of joy and gratitude. Memories came flooding in...

Unequally Yoked

The birth of a son!! What exhilarating happiness Eunice felt as she held this precious gift from God. At the same time, she was sobered knowing that his spiritual training would mostly be her responsibility. What joy she felt, seeing how proudly her handsome Greek husband looked at the tiny bundle in her arms. What thankfulness that her mother—now a grandmother—was there to support and strengthen her, to pray with her. She needed to rely more on God than she ever had. Naively, Eunice had thought that the addition of a child to their mixed marriage would produce little conflict. Her husband's Greek and heathen background were seemingly unimportant to him while her own Jewish faith in the one true God and his holy Scriptures was preeminent. She was unprepared for his reaction as she suggested the name *Timothy,* signifying "one who fears God." She could still remember being stunned by her husband's complete resistance to circumcising their son on the eighth day according to Jewish law. Wisely, Grandmother Lois had urged her to entrust this baby son to God and prayerfully and willingly to be submissive to her husband. Eunice couldn't help smiling as she realized how many times she had put that same advice into practice. How powerfully God had answered and honored those prayers and actions!

Train Up a Child

As Eunice recalled those early days of Timothy's life, she remembered the pact she and Lois had made to do all within their power to train him in the fear of God and in the knowledge of the Scriptures. A Jewish boy formally began to study the Old Testament at age five, but Timothy was taught by his mother and grandmother at home at a much earlier age. During those years, young Timothy had frequent bouts of illness and, yet, was never too weak to enjoy hearing the Scriptures read. It delighted him to surprise Eunice and Lois by reciting the scriptures he had committed to memory! Even his father, though an unbeliever, was amazed and inwardly impressed by his son's knowledge and zeal.

Mothers' prayers for their children are probably the most consistent requests brought to God. Certainly this was true for Eunice.

Often she and Lois would plead together for wisdom, guidance and extra help so they could train Timothy to be his best for God. She felt her limitations as a woman married to an unbeliever. She knew Timothy needed a strong spiritual male influence. She saw gaps in his development, especially due to his physical illnesses that weakened him and caused him to withdraw at times. Little had she known how God would meet those needs.

Changed for Eternity

In her mind's eye she could see Paul and Barnabas in the marketplace as clearly as if it were yesterday. Eunice and her mother had just gotten there when they saw a huge crowd of people shouting, "The gods Zeus and Hermes have come down to us in human form!" Immediately, two men rushed out of the crowd tearing their clothes crying out, "Why are you doing this? We too are only men, human like you. We are bringing you good news, telling you to turn from these worthless things to the living God" (Acts 14:15).

On hearing those words, Eunice and Lois worked their way to the front of the crowd, eager to hear what these men had to say about "the living God." What they heard struck their hearts as nothing ever had. THE MESSIAH—their long-awaited Messiah had come! Jesus of Nazareth came teaching and healing only to be betrayed and crucified!

Tears filled Eunice's eyes as she remembered Paul's convicting words about each person's sin being responsible for the crucifying of the Son of God. When that startling reality hit her, she could hardly breathe. She was guilty. What could she do? Yet, thankfully, Paul had told of Jesus' burial and then his incredible resurrection three days later, and hope entered her heart. For Lois and Eunice, time stopped until they made that decision of decisions—Jesus would be their Lord! They would be disciples! Repenting of all their sins, they were baptized into Jesus—into the very kingdom of God! Their lives had forever been changed.

And Timothy? She should have known there would be no way to hold him back. His love for the Scriptures and for God had prepared him to hear Paul's message. Timothy had seen his mother's and grandmother's tears of joy and heard the great news about Jesus. He saw their faith in action and saw changes in their lives like never before. He had to meet Paul and Barnabas. It wasn't hard to find them—just look for the crowd.

What a message! What boldness! What courage! Timothy had never heard a man speak with such forceful convictions. Eunice would never forget what happened next. She and her mother had been right behind Timothy, when out of the crowd, angry Jews from Antioch and Iconium pushed toward Paul. Their taunts and jeers and threats grew louder and spread like wildfire, turning the crowd into an angry mob. They shoved and dragged Paul outside the city where they viciously stoned him.

As quickly as the mob had gathered, it dispersed leaving the seemingly dead Paul in the dirt. The disciples surrounded the body. Before they could begin to mourn his death, Paul got up from the ground. Unbelievable! Miraculous! The disciples were jumping for joy, crying, praising and thanking God and hugging Paul all at once. After the initial exuberance, Timothy felt burning tears of shame rolling down his face as he realized his own fear, his lack of faith, his lack of boldness in the face of danger. Eunice knew he was experiencing the same heart-rending awareness of his sins that she had felt when Paul had preached about the cross of Jesus. Nothing could stop him. Timothy—her young son, her young man—became a disciple. Paul's words, "We must go through many hardships to enter the kingdom of God" (Acts 14:22) would be indelibly stamped on their hearts and minds.

God's Answers

Was it just a few weeks ago that Paul had come back to Lystra? So much had happened in a short span of time. Eunice stood in awe of how God had answered her prayers. She could not have asked for a more spiritual man than Paul to disciple her son. Paul knew Timothy's weaknesses, but he saw his potential and had great vision for him. Timothy's eagerness to accompany Paul on his travels was evidence that God had answered prayers for growth in his boldness and courage. Timothy certainly had seen firsthand what hardships meant. And Timothy's circumcision—it hadn't happened when he was eight days old, but it did happen before he left with Paul. God used even that to help her trust his timing. And Timothy certainly learned a new level of trust in God—and in Paul, who did the circumcising (Acts 16:3)!

Eunice turned back to the house after Paul and Timothy disappeared from her sight. Lois came to meet her. As they embraced, no words were spoken. Their tears came again, and in their hearts they shared a deeper faith than ever. Somehow they knew this faith, this trust would be tried and tested in the months and years to come. They could be at peace; their son/grandson was in good hands—Paul's, and most of all—God's!

Times of Surrender

Eunice and Lois have come alive through my study. I identify with Eunice as a mother; I identify with Lois as a grandmother. What models of faith they both are! When I thought of Eunice and Lois in years past, I was inspired by their training of Timothy from infancy. Their example especially influenced me in my years of motherhood when our three girls, Staci, Kristi and Keri were young. My own parents instilled in me a love for God and his Word from an early age, and I wanted to do that for our girls. Memorizing Bible verses was a regular part of our family devotionals and meal times together. Al, the girls and I would take turns quizzing each other, and we grew together.

Probably the most convicting aspect of Eunice and Lois' lives was their faith. When I have read 2 Timothy 4:5—Paul's words to Timothy of his "sincere faith which first lived in your grandmother Lois and in your mother Eunice"—I have thought in terms of their faith to become disciples and that faith influencing Timothy. Digging deeper into the lives of Timothy, Eunice and Lois has challenged me profoundly as I have thought of the circumstances in which a mother's and grandmother's faith would be tested the most. To realize for the first time that Eunice probably witnessed Paul's stoning in Acts 14; and then later agreed to her teenage son traveling with that same man, fully understanding the persecutions that would face them, *challenged me to the core!* Today, some of us have difficulty "letting go" of our children as they go to school for the first time or spend a night away from us.

A point in my life when I could especially identify with Eunice occurred several years ago when all three of our girls left us in Boston about the same time to pursue mission opportunities around the world. I remember the feelings of concern, loneliness and a certain "emptiness" with all our daughters out of reach. At the same time, I was thankful for the opportunities each of them would have. For me it was a time of growing and maturing as I "untied the apron strings"—one of many times to surrender our girls to God.

My own mother has been a great example to me through the years as she and my dad willingly and prayerfully supported our moving from Texas to Boston (with their only grandchildren). I remembered that model as our daughter Staci and her husband, Andy, moved to Italy. That challenged the "almost-grandmother" role in me, because Staci was pregnant and would deliver our first grandchild in an Italian hospital. God continues to prove his love and care for us and honors our faith and surrender to him. He has blessed us with a beautiful granddaughter, Kiara, now a year old and a little closer to us in Boston.

God has placed so much power in the hands of women—to build up or to tear down. Through the years I have developed what I call my "open-hands prayer." As fear, anxiety and worry tempt me, I consciously, physically open my hands in prayer to God, releasing everything to his care and will. There are times when the struggle to control is so strong that I have to open my hands again and again to surrender fully.

Whether mothers, grandmothers, wives or singles, the challenge is to be faithful women who will continually surrender every area of our lives to God. Now hundreds of years later, though very little was written about them, the example of Eunice and Lois motivates and inspires us like never before!

Gloria Baird
Los Angeles, USA

 Which word describes your approach to life—control or surrender? What or how do you need to surrender today?

application questions on page 183

28

PHILIP'S DAUGHTERS
Chosen by God

Acts 21:7-9

On the Day of Pentecost, the inaugural day of the church, Peter quoted Joel the prophet: "In the last days, God says, I will pour out my spirit on all people. Your sons and daughters will prophesy...." The Spirit moved in powerful ways, confirming and establishing the truth of the gospel. Philip the evangelist realized the fulfillment of Joel's prophesy in quadruplicate—all four of his unmarried daughters prophesied. What a joy they must have been to their Christ-centered father.

◆

Leaving the next day, we reached Caesarea and stayed at the house of Philip the evangelist, one of the Seven. He had four unmarried daughters who prophesied (Acts 21:8-9).

How privileged these four women were to have such a rich heritage in the kingdom! Like Timothy, they were chosen from infancy to know the Scripture. They were daughters of the evangelist Philip—the same Philip who was one of the Seven chosen to serve the church in Acts 6:3-5:

"Brothers, choose seven men from among you who are known to be full of the Spirit and wisdom..." They chose Stephen, a man full of the Holy Spirit; also Philip...

Did Philip have any of his little daughters at this point in time? We do not know. We do know that one of the chosen, Stephen, was stoned to death for his faith. Then we read in Acts 8 that godly men mourned and buried Stephen, and as the church was scattered, "Philip went down to a city in Samaria and proclaimed the Christ there" (Acts 8:5). Philip must have been deeply moved by the death of Stephen. Perhaps that event motivated him all the more to choose to use his life for God.

Were any of these daughters around in the early days in Samaria? Did they see Simon Magus the Sorcerer following their dad everywhere (Acts 8:13)? Did Simon see Philip playing with his children and still miss the point that love is the greatest power? Were the girls there when the apostles Peter and John came to Samaria and Peter exposed Simon's heart? Did they see the apostles pray, and did they see them lay hands and impart the Holy Spirit?

Were the girls born after their father preached to and baptized the Ethiopian official? It was their father who had followed the Holy Spirit's direction to approach the chariot and ask, "Do you understand what you are reading?" in Acts 8:30. He must have asked that same question as he later taught his own daughters the Scriptures. Of course the girls were grown by the time Paul and Luke stayed at their home in Samaria en route to Jerusalem in Acts 21. By that time, the girls had all chosen to follow God.

We do not know what experiences the girls had growing up. We do not even know who Philip's wife was. It is a testimony to God at work in Philip's life that, while Philip was forcefully advancing the kingdom, he raised up not one or two, but *four* daughters who chose to follow in his footsteps in also advancing the kingdom. While the Word does not tell us specifically how he did this, his example is certainly an upward call to us in the kingdom to be spiritual leaders who lead our own children to God.

Perhaps their father's example of bringing about amazing changes in people's lives drew these women to want to do God's will. Yet, surely that example alone would not have been enough. Philip must also have been living out his example at home— helping each of them to personally understand "the good news about Jesus" (Acts 8:35).

The Bible says that the girls were unmarried. It seems as though they were old enough to be married, but for some reason they were not. Either they personally had chosen not to marry, or God had chosen for them not to marry. Perhaps each had chosen to live out the principle of 1 Corinthians 7:35 that a single woman can "live in undivided devotion to the Lord." Perhaps marrying and having children was in their future, but not at the present time. We only know that their marital status was single when they were referred to in Acts 9. But what were these women doing? They were prophesying. They were not fretting about their futures; they were not fearing that they were overlooked by God—they were being used by God!

When I think of Philip's daughters, I am reminded of Proverbs 21:26 (Revised Standard Version):

> All day long the wicked covets
> but the righteous gives and does not hold back.

They could have chosen to "covet," to ask, "Why is it that others get to marry and start families and we don't?" If they had, they would have begun to withhold from God—holding back their hearts, their thoughts, their time, their treasure. Left unchecked, their thoughts could have led to sneaking around and finding men outside the kingdom who would be with them. But these women, like their father, were surrendered to God's will. They believed they were chosen to be holy—not without sin, but "set apart for God's use." That is why God could use them to tell his words to others. God chose to give them the gift of prophecy, which involves communicating with others to help them know and follow God.

When Paul and Luke arrived, these women must have been thrilled to meet them in person. Perhaps this is when they received their gift. They must have been blessed abundantly. Choosing to be spiritual enabled these women to find God's will and to be content and effective in their current life situation.

Personally Chosen

I was unmarried in the kingdom for a long time. When my older sister, Sheila, married Tom Jones after her junior year of college, I assumed that my future would be similar: I would finish college and then marry. Not so!

Looking back, I thank God for the plans he had "to prosper me and not to harm me and to give me hope and a future." (Jeremiah 29:11). I moved to Florida and became a disciple in Tallahassee at age 21. Bruce Williams, now an elder in the Los Angeles church, baptized me into Christ, and I worked as a ministry intern in the campus ministry that he led. I loved the work of the ministry, and those were productive, fruitful years for me. God began using Bruce and Robyn Williams to mold and shape my character and heart. I prayed that God would send the perfect man for me, but I promised God that I would trust his timing and his decision. I now know that God had a plan for me—personally. He loved me personally, just as he loved Philip's daughters personally, and just as he loves *you* personally.

I cherish the memory of my physical father, Taylor. He loved me deeply and would do anything within his power to make me happy (just as I now feel about my own children!). I often thought, *He loves me so much that if there were any way he could possibly create someone just for me, he'd do it in a heartbeat.* But, he had neither the wisdom nor the power. But my heavenly Father had (and has!) both. God knew what was best for me. My relationship with God made my life rich and full. Yet I asked God to please give me a companion who would not move away or marry someone else and who would help me to serve God even more.

I remember going home to family reunions. I always went home prayerful that I could let my light shine and be an example...and then some relative would say—would *always* say—"Do you have any prospects?" I would think of the passage when Isaac asked Abraham where the ram for sacrifice was, and Abraham replied that the LORD would provide. I believed that God would provide whatever was helpful and best in my life. Mostly I held onto that belief, but there were low times when I needed help with my faith.

Once I had traveled home to North Alabama to a family gathering. I sat outside in my car, not really wanting to go in. I knew that everyone was there with all the new spouses and babies. As I sat in my car that night, my Dad came out and talked with me for awhile. He told me how he felt during Word War II when he missed Mom but still had to give to other people. He reminded me that God knows what is best for me and that I must trust him, which helped me to remember that I had chosen to live for God. I knew at my baptism that I was chosen, but for the rest of my Christian walk, I would need to keep on choosing. That night I chose to be a giver. I went in. I played my guitar and shared what God was doing in my life and on the campuses in Florida.

Then one day when I was 30 years old, I met John Bringardner, the man I would eventually marry. I first saw him in the elevator in the Florida state capitol building on my way to a Bible discussion group on the 32 floor. I still remember the comment he made during the study and how my heart pounded.

Our second date was on his birthday—he turned 23! I wondered if he knew how old I was. He did and it never mattered. He was the one for me. After being a maid of honor in sixteen weddings, I married the man of my dreams.

God's plan was that I be single for many years in the kingdom and then, in his time, to have for a husband the man who would help me serve him even better! I wondered if I could have children, and then God gave us three! Who would have thought that God would have picked John for me and that I would have our third child when I was forty years old living in Bangkok, Thailand?!

We never know what our future holds. We must only decide, like Philip's daughters, to be useful in God's service. The key is then to keep on choosing to be spiritual. Though Philip must have been a great inspiration to his girls to stay spiritual, perhaps they were also inspired by their mom, or special friends who were disciples. Who is it for you? I remember many times God used other disciples to help me. Their advice helped me keep my spiritual perspective and make those single years happy and fruitful times.

My sister once told me, "You need the best soldier to go into battle with."

My dad said, "Marry someone who will help you get to heaven."

And about my future relationship, one of my best friends at that time, Martha Peacock, said, "You should both believe you got the best deal!"

In conclusion, what I learned from Philip's daughters and from God's plan for my life is this: Be proud to be chosen to be a daughter of God! Be spiritual! Be a giver! And let others help you. These sisters chose to embrace God's purpose. And then he chose to use them in a special way in the kingdom by giving them the gift of prophecy. Are you choosing to embrace God's purpose? Surely, though we no longer can receive miraculous gifts, there are gifts he is waiting to give you to use for him. You must choose—for you, too, are "chosen by God."

I chose to trust and serve our God, He gave me the soldier I needed for every battle and the man who would help me get to heaven. By choosing to rely on God, I know I got the best deal!

Emily Bringardner
Los Angeles, USA

Read Psalm 73. Does earth have anything that you desire besides God? What? What things most tempt you to be discontented? What are you tempted to covet in others in or out of the kingdom? How are you/can you learn contentedness in the face of these temptations?

application questions on page 183

29

PHOEBE
Simply a Servant

Romans 16:1-2

Paul was a Jewish teacher who was comfortable in the presence of women. He realized they were coheirs with him of the blessings offered by Jesus (Galatians 3:28-29; Ephesians 3:6). Both Jewish and Greek women were among his friends, supporters and coworkers.

On his second missionary journey, Paul spent eighteen months in Corinth. There he met and teamed up with Priscilla and Aquila. Six miles from Corinth, on the coast of the Mediterranean, or Great Sea, a church was also established in Cenchrea. It was from that port Paul and his two friends set sail for Ephesus after leaving Corinth. Before sailing he had his hair cut as a result of a vow he had taken. (Nazirite vows were temporary in nature and usually ended with the shaving of the head.)

Upon his return to this area about five years later, in all likelihood he entrusted the delivery of his letter to the Roman Christians to a servant of the church in Cenchrea. She was one of the special sisters in his life.

◆

How honored she felt! What a privilege it would be to visit the brothers and sisters in Rome and see them face to face. Not only that, but to be chosen to hand deliver the letter the apostle Paul had written to them was an opportunity of a lifetime. She felt a sense of destiny as she excitedly made plans to make the long journey from Cenchrea to Rome. It would be a very difficult trip to make, and Phoebe was well aware of the dangers, especially as a woman. In all likelihood, she was experienced in travel and had made similar journeys, so she knew what she was undertaking. And yet, the joy of being able to serve God, and Paul, in this capacity, must have thrilled her beyond words.

Phoebe was no ordinary woman. She was different! There were few sisters like Phoebe in the kingdom, and few women like her in the world. She had a servant's heart. And, for this, she is remembered by all.

A New Life

Phoebe was from the city of Cenchrea. Like every major seaport, it was a city known for being a commercial center as well as a flagrantly wicked place. It seems that Phoebe was a prominent and influential woman, and blessed with material wealth as well. No doubt, she was ambitious and had always wanted to be someone who would have a great impact on others, but the world and her pursuits had left her empty, purposeless and lonely. Although she had accomplished much, deep inside she knew there was something more, something greater.

She found that "something" when the gospel spread from Corinth to Cenchrea. Phoebe found Jesus, and her life changed drastically. Her desires, motives, dreams and ambitions were totally transformed. No longer was she pursuing her own plans; now she was surrendered to Jesus and to his plans for her life. She had, no doubt, been influenced by other prominent women, such as Priscilla, from Corinth. Phoebe would have respected Priscilla and admired the way God used her powerfully to impact other women to know and love Jesus. Phoebe was genuinely grateful for her salvation and for the talents and material blessings that God had given to her. Phoebe's desire was that God would use her to help others. And that is what he did. All of the brothers and sisters in Cenchrea loved Phoebe deeply because she helped so many of them.

A Giver

Phoebe's home was always open to the brothers and sisters and her hospitality was exemplary. She was someone who warmed the hearts of all because she delighted in meeting needs and freely giving to others what God had given her. Whether it was a warm meal, encouraging words, acts of kindness, helping the sick, or giving financially, Phoebe was always looking for ways to serve. She had learned the secret of our Savior—that the greatest of all is the servant of all. Phoebe allowed God to take her talents and influence to benefit the kingdom in every way. In her heart, she knew it was the very least she could do to thank him.

We can know, as with anyone, there were days when Phoebe was tempted to ask herself the questions, *"What about me?"* and *"When will I get some time for myself?"* It was also at this time that she would look back at her old life, when she was in the driver's seat, and miss that sense of control. But, she very quickly remembered where that control had led her and how the selfish lifestyle of the "rich and famous" had left her desolate within. No, never would she forget what she had been saved from. Phoebe had learned to consider others better than herself and that the greatest joy in life comes from giving, not getting. And, in her heart, she knew she could never give more than God had given.

An Ambassador

And now, the fruit of her heart and character had prompted the apostle Paul to choose her to be his ambassador to Rome. She would be his forerunner to the Christians there, and her life would be a witness to his as she delivered Paul's most powerful epistle. Paul had a deep sense of respect for her and an appreciation for all that she had done to help him personally. As Paul had not yet been to Rome, he, no doubt, had full confidence that Phoebe would represent him well and that the brothers and sisters in Rome would be changed by her life and example. She was a woman of impact who left an indelible impression on all she met.

Eager to Serve

What a special sister Phoebe was, and how wonderful it will be to meet her in heaven. Can you imagine spending a day with her as she tirelessly served others, helping to meet many needs as she denied herself? Phoebe's life and example inspires me to be a greater servant! When I consider what I want others to remember and commend me for, there is no question that I want to be remembered as a servant of Jesus.

I became a Christian when I was 16 years old. If you had asked my family, "What comes to mind when you think of Maria?" no one would have responded by saying that I was a servant. Not even close! "Self-centered" would have been the likely response. As it has been said, "Who we are at home is who we are." Well, let's just say I wrote the book on selfishness. I was always thinking about what I wanted and how I could get it, regardless of who it hurt. The people I loved the most, my family, were the ones who suffered the most from my selfishness. I can still remember the many fights I had and the angry words exchanged because I wasn't getting my way. Six months before I became a Christian, my selfishness led me to a fit of rage in an argument with my mother and sister. It resulted in my putting my hand through a window. I was reminded of my selfishness daily because the stitches left me unable to use my hand. My doctor told me to lie and tell others that I cut it on a broken glass while washing dishes. But, I knew the truth. And so did God. I was selfish!

I'm so grateful my older brother invited me to a Bible discussion and got me into the Bible. The Word of God opened my eyes as I saw Jesus and his selflessness on the cross. I was so convicted of my selfishness and all the ways I had hurt others. The way I viewed my family and school friends totally changed. I genuinely wanted to put the needs of others above my own, and it felt so good! Finally, I could love others from the heart without ulterior motives. Jesus was teaching and preparing me to serve in ways much greater than I ever imagined.

Now, in the full-time ministry with four small children, there is no shortage of needs to meet. They are everywhere, constantly. My challenge now is to joyously, rather than anxiously, seek to serve and meet the needs around me. At times, I forget who I'm serving, and I get resentful if I feel unappreciated by someone. When I have Phoebe's heart, I remember who I'm serving and why. It's at those times that I remember the greatest example of service: Jesus on the cross. When I'm grateful for all God has done for me, I'm eager to serve, and it's not a burden, but a joy.

It's so easy and so very natural to be selfish. It takes the heart of Jesus to be a servant. Servants like Phoebe are rare and treasured. I want to be in her company, to the glory of God!

Maria Rogers
Boston, USA

 FOCUS In what ways do you need to change to be commended as a servant?

application questions on page 184

BIBLIOGRAPHY

Chestnutt, Randall D., "Jewish Women in the Greco-Roman Era." *Essays on Women in Earliest Christianity*. Ed. Carroll Osburn. Joplin, Missouri: College Press, 1993. 93-130.

Deen, Edith. *All of the Women of the Bible*. New York: Harper and Row, 1955.

Deen, Edith. *The Bible's Legacy for Womanhood*. Garden City, New York: Doubleday and Company, Inc., 1969.

Edersheim, Alfred. *The Life and Times of Jesus the Messiah*. Peabody, Massachusetts: Hendrickson, 1993.

Edersheim, Alfred. *Sketches of Jewish Social Life,* updated edition. Peabody, Massachusetts: Hendrickson Publishers, 1994.

Gaertner, Dennis. *The College Press NIV Commentary*. Joplin, Missouri: College Press, 1993.

Lockyer, Herbert. *All the Women of the Bible*. Grand Rapids, Michigan: Zondervan, 1967.

NIV Study Bible. Grand Rapids, Michigan: Zondervan, 1985.

Schurer, Emil. *A History of the Jewish People in the Times of Jesus Christ*. 1890. Peabody, Massachusetts: Hendrickson Publishers, 1994.

APPLICATION
Your Personal Response

1 Elizabeth

1. Do you ever doubt God's promises to you? How do you deal with that doubt?

2. Elizabeth shared her heart with Mary. Who do you share your heart with? What fears do you have about being open?

3. What does it mean to you that Jesus has come to your life? Do you respond as Elizabeth and John the Baptist did?

4. In what situations are you tempted to be competitive?

5. Do you try so hard to look "good" that you actually become dishonest?

2 Mary, Mother of Jesus

1. What kind of challenges would keep you from completely surrendering to God's plan?

2. Mary's heart was willing to accept God's gift and then to give the gift back. How easy is it for you to give back to God what he has blessed you with?

3. What dreams do you have for your life? Are they God's dreams for you?

4. Are you willing to do whatever it takes to see God's dream for your life fulfilled?

3 Anna the Prophetess

1. What is your attitude toward daily miracles? Are you thankful for the ways God is working in your life every day, or are you only looking for "big," every-once-in-a-while miracles? Anna was content in her daily celebration of God in her life.

2. Are you bored and burdened, or caught up in "external" spiritual success only? Or are you able to have peace in your heart

because you are daily seeking to do God's will (even if you are in bed with the flu and can't do all the "works" you normally do)?

3.   Anna stayed focused and faithful to God even when surrounded by turbulent happenings. How well do you do in staying focused and faithful when life is blurring around you?

4.   Are your thoughts mostly self-centered or God-centered? When you are going through some difficulty, is your response "Why is this happening to me?" or "How can God work through this to bring glory to his name?"?

5.   Do you need to shed any of the following "shells": ambition, material accumulations, ego, pride, false ambition, masks and armor? As you shed more and more shells, what does God promise you?

4 Mary Magdalene

1.   How does Mary Magdalene's life exemplify the life of a disciple?

2.   Discuss gratitude as the foundation of devotion and sacrifice. How grateful are you?

3.   Mary Magdalene had a number of great friends in her life. Discuss your own friendships. What kind of friend are you, and what kind of friendships do you have?

4.   What kind of servant are you? How do you respond when your service goes unnoticed or unheralded?

5.   Mary Magdalene's devotion to Jesus did not fade with the passage of time. How long have you been a disciple of Jesus? Has your love and eagerness to serve deepened with time, or has it slowly ebbed over the months and years?

5 Herodias

1.   How do you react when confronted about your sin? Do you look for reasons and excuses to justify your action or attitude? Or do you seek out correction and challenge?

2. If you are married, are you submissive to your husband's decisions? Or is your mind busy trying to figure out ways to buy what you want or to schedule things the way that you want or to live exactly where you want? Do you allow your husband's opinions and ideas to influence your way of thinking? Or are you holding on to your point of view with all of your heart and waiting for the next opportunity to prove your point?

3. What would your children tell others about you? Do they "arise and call you blessed?" (Proverbs 31:28). Would they say that you are superlatively happy and so much fun to be around? Are they learning about God's peace "which transcends all understanding" (Philippians 4:7) from their mother?

4. Who are you blaming for a current problem or failure in your life? What hurt or difficulty lies unresolved and unforgiven in your heart? Do you think that you are above being controlled by these sinful thoughts and attitudes? If the Spirit is showing you something to repent of, what is your next step?

5. Are you daily grateful for God's grace? Remember how much he loves you and how eager he is to forgive you and cleanse you. He longed to even have Herodias as his daughter. You *are* his daughter.

6 Sinful Woman

1. When she heard that Jesus was eating at the Pharisee's house, the sinful woman did not hesitate to go to him. Would you have hesitated? Why?

2. When was the last time you cried over your sin?

3. What could you change in your life to come to God more like this sinful woman came—humbly and loving much?

4. Do you ever doubt that you have been given the same blessings that Jesus promised to this woman (forgiveness of sins, salvation)? Why?

7 Bleeding Woman

1. After 12 years of suffering, this woman's faith was still alive. How do you respond to prolonged trials? How does it affect your faith?

2. This woman had to push through a crowd. What do you have to push through daily to get to Jesus?

3. Are there any areas of your life with which you don't fully trust God? (i.e. dating relationships, children, finances, character changes)

4. Is it easier for you to have others need and depend on you or for you to need and depend on others? Why?

8 Widow of Nain

1. What is "hardship" to you?

2. What is the first thing you do when you are faced with hardship?

3. What are some ways you might get in God's way?

4. How do you respond to someone else's trials and struggles?

5. What is your reaction when God's will is different from what you wanted?

9 Mary of Bethany

1. Looking back at the past week, what has been the priority of your life?

2. Do the trials and tragedies of life drive you closer to Jesus or farther away?

3. What is the most passionate action you have taken for God lately? Do you avoid embarrassing ways of displaying your love for Jesus?

4. Who would your closest friend say you are more like, Mary or Martha?

10 Martha

1. Think of the qualities of Martha's heart that made her teachable. Compare these to the qualities of your own heart. Ask a few close friends if they consider you as teachable as Martha and if you are a great friend to them. Let them grade you on a scale of 1 to 5, 5 being awesome!

2. List two of your strengths. List one major weakness that you want to change, and write out a plan as to how you will change it.

3. Think of Martha's ability to impact not only Jesus, but her family and village. Write out a list of names of people whom you want to impact for the kingdom. What attributes of Martha's character do you need to imitate to see them become disciples?

4. Send a card to the women who have discipled you during your Christian life. Express your gratitude for them and their leadership.

11 Samaritan Woman

1. When you have a problem, is it your tendency to think you can handle it on your own, or do you seek help and get advice?

2. Are there sins in your past that you won't even let yourself think about because they're still too painful? Have you truly given everything over to God?

3. How would you feel being known as the Floridian woman or the Los Angeles woman or maybe the Chinese woman? We really don't know who the Samaritan woman was. Do a pride check.

4. Are you a conflict avoider? Do you see that as a sin?

5. Does your gratitude toward Jesus show in the lives you touch every day?

12 Joanna

1. What circumstances can threaten your perseverance? Your gratitude? Your joy?

2. How are you impacted by the faith of your spouse or close friend?

3. What is your attitude toward sacrificing for Jesus and his kingdom?

4. How do you respond if you do not feel respected by another person? By a leader?

13 Widow at the Temple

1. This poor woman gave beyond what she could see. What limits have you set on giving? What can you do to become radical in your giving?

2. The widow's giving came from the overflow of the heart. What motivates you to give?

3. Make a list of as many things as you can think of that have been given to you by God. How quickly can you think of 50 things? As you look at this list, what impact does it have on your heart and your giving?

4. What has examining your giving taught you about your heart? What have you decided to change?

14 Mother of the Blind Man

1. What do you fear most? How does this show a lack of trust in God?

2. When have you compromised your convictions because of the fear of how someone else might react?

3. Do you ever feel paralyzed by your fears? How would you "disciple" yourself to confront these areas in your life?

4. What are you worried about? Is there anything you can do about it today? If yes, what will you do and when will you do it? If no, decide to leave it up to God to do as he sees best.

15 Syrophoenician Woman

1. The Syrophoenician woman was desperate to get her daughter healed because she loved her. Do you love the women in your life as you would a daughter or a sister?

2. This pagan knew that Jesus was the only hope she had for saving her daughter. Do you really believe that Jesus is your only hope? The only hope for all of the world to be saved? Or has Christianity become a religion, a club, a way of life?

3. Think for a moment how you would have responded to the apostles and to Jesus if you had been in her situation. Would you have been arrogant or insecure or both? When are the times that you struggle with arrogance/insecurity now? What have you learned from this woman to help you change?

4. Our pagan friend was commended for her faith by Jesus. What circumstances cause you to give up? Memorize some promises of God, and decide to be known as a woman of great faith.

16 Pilate's Wife

1. Pilate's wife had a conviction that Jesus was innocent. Make a list of convictions that you have.

2. In what ways can you be more responsible and have a greater impact on those around you?

3. Do you have the courage to risk your relationships, reputation and comfort to stand up for what is right?

4. Would God be pleased with your heart today? To remind you of what kind of heart is pleasing to God, make a list of verses which talk about the heart.

17 Sapphira

1. What possessions or pleasures are you afraid you will lose if you decide to give more time or money to God and people?

2. Do you ever give just because it is expected? To "save face"?

3. Neither Ananias nor Sapphira influenced each other for good. When you feel the pressure to compromise your convictions, what helps you stand firm?

4. Have you ever been tempted to lead out of a desire for position rather than a desire to serve?

5. Do people know the battles you are fighting inside?

18 Mary, Mother of John Mark

1. Mary really regarded the kingdom of God as her family. Discuss what the kingdom means to you. What is one new way you can show your love for God's family?

2. Mothers, how are you doing in trusting God's care for each of your children? Do you see their need for other disciples in their lives?

3. The disciples gathered for prayer and were surprised at the quick answer they received. Discuss the last time you were amazed at an "unexpected" answer to prayer.

4. There was only one verse referring specifically to Mary, yet we have learned a lot about her by digging deeply into the Word. How can you dig deeper in your personal study time?

19 Rhoda

1. How much do you believe when you pray? Do you just say what you wish would happen? Or do you believe your prayers will make a difference?

2. Do your convictions stand the test of criticism, even from other disciples?

3. What do you think to yourself as you pray for the same thing over and over? Do you believe that God hears you?

4. Answered prayer builds our faith. Do you keep up with your prayers to know if they are answered? How does it affect you when someone shares an answered prayer with you?

20 Salome, Mother of James and John

1. How can you be rightly ambitious about your children's spiritual growth? About your own spiritual growth?

2. What kind of response do you generally have when corrected or discipled in the area of parenting? In other areas?

3. In what ways are you overprotective with your children, not allowing them to mature? With young Christians?

4. What fears and anxieties weigh you down when it comes to your children's physical and spiritual well-being? Your own well-being?

21 Dorcas

1. How often do you take it upon yourself to help a poor person? Do you wait for church-planned activities to do something for the poor, or do you initiate yourself?

2. What would you change in your daily schedule to be more like Dorcas?

3. Examine your relationships in the church. If you died tomorrow, would the disciples and others you have helped react in the same way as they did at Dorcas' funeral? Why or why not?

4. What is your reputation in the church today in the area of helping others? Do you want to change it? How will you change it?

22 Lydia

1. Are you fearful of challenges? Of undertaking new responsibilities? How will you deal with this fear?

2. Do leaders intimidate you? How can you get to know them better?

3. Are you growing in your trust in God? How?

4. It is easy to seek "the ministry" or "conversions" rather than God. How can you avoid falling into this trap? How will you seek God more deeply?

23 Priscilla

1. Are your friendships close enough and spiritual enough to protect you from burnout?

2. In what areas might you tend to burn out? How will you stay committed?

3. Are you a team player? Do you say what you are thinking in discussions? If you are married, how well do you work with your husband?

4. Paul was Priscilla and Aquila's hero. Do you have a spiritual hero? What do you specifically learn from him or her?

24 Drusilla and Bernice

1. How does your family background affect you today? Do you ever blame your sins and character weaknesses on your background?

2. Are you more likely to focus on your own fears and inadequacies or on people's needs and God's power?

3. What convictions do you need to deepen to become a woman who would never hesitate to share her faith?

4. When we die to our old self, we will no longer regard anyone "from a worldly point of view" (2 Corinthians 5:16). What worldly point of view keeps you from loving people enough to give them a chance to know God?

25 Weak-Willed Women

1. Are there Bible doctrines that you could be swayed on because you are not sure what you believe? (Read Ephesians 4:14.) Commit yourself to studying these out until you have firm convictions.

2. Can you have an open mind and still have deep convictions? Why or why not?

3. In what areas of your life are you weak-willed? What sins are hardest for you to overcome?

4. How can you become more disciplined in your thinking? In your actions?

26 Euodia and Syntyche

1. How do you typically handle conflict? Ignore it and hope it will go away, or go after resolving it?

2. What fears do you have when you experience a conflict with someone?

3. What scriptural principles do you apply in situations of conflict?

4. Are you the one who initiates to resolve conflict, or do you wait for the other person?

27 Eunice and Lois

1. For mothers:

    In what specific ways are you training your children? What do they see in your example?

    How are you preparing to "untie the apron strings"?

    How do you encourage your children when they have to sacrifice for the sake of Jesus and the kingdom?

2. If you are single and hope to have children one day, what did you learn about being a mother from these women?

3. What excuses are you tempted to make when you do not handle a situation faithfully?

4. Describe a time when you went through a hardship or struggle victoriously.

28 Philip's Daughters

1. Has your appreciation for the kingdom increased or decreased the longer you have been a disciple? How are your relationships with those who have been in the kingdom for a long time (or at least longer than you have been)? What types of things can you learn from them?

2. Think about your kingdom dreams. (Do you have some?) Are you fired-up about your role in the kingdom? God wants to use each and every one of us to help others. Do you see God at work in your life and ministry?

3. When things aren't going as we had hoped, as women we can tend to become negative and critical, and fill our conversations with whining and complaining. How can you fight against this temptation? What great things have you seen God do for you in the past? Recently?

4. If you are single, what was the greatest lesson of encouragement that you learned from reading this chapter?

29 Phoebe

1. How are you striving to serve others around you on a daily basis?

2. In which areas of your life can you be selfish?

3. What motivates you when you serve?

4. What inspires you the most about Phoebe's life?

5. Phoebe won the hearts of many. What enabled her to do this? Do you have these qualities? How can you grow?

THE EDITORS

Sheila Presley Jones holds certification for teaching secondary English and serves as associate editor of Discipleship Publications International. She and her husband, Tom, who serves as the editor-in-chief for DPI, have lived in the Boston area for eight years. They have three daughters, all committed disciples. She and her husband have worked with churches in four states, leading evangelistic efforts and numerous workshops on marriage, family and spiritual growth.

Linda Tucker Brumley is a California native now living in Seattle. In the full-time ministry for the past eight years, she now serves as women's ministry leader in the church where her husband, Ron, is an elder. They have four grown children who are all disciples. For many years Linda has studied and taught the Bible both to small and large groups. She has special expertise in Old Testament study and has prepared materials specifically in this area for children's education programs.

Other Resources Available from DPI

She Shall Be Called Woman - Volume 1
Old Testament Women
edited by Sheila Jones and Linda Brumley

9 to 5 and Spiritually Alive
by Sheila Jones

The Victory of Surrender
by Gordon Ferguson

Raising Awesome Kids in Troubled Times
by Sam and Geri Laing

Mind Change: The Overcomer's Handbook
by Thomas Jones

The Disciple's Wedding
Planning a wedding that gives glory to God
by Nancy Orr

Friend & Lovers
by Sam and Geri Laing

Our Beginning
by Kay Summers McKean

The Fine Art of Hospitality
edited by Sheila Jones
The Fine Art of Hospitality Handbook
edited by Sheila Jones and Betty Dyson
TWO-BOOK SET

Real God, Real Women
by Kay Summers McKean

Working 9 to 5
by Madaline Evans, Debbie Miller,
Sheila Jones and Kim Walters

For more information about ordering these
and many other resources from DPI, call
1-888-DPI-BOOK
or from outside the US:
781-937-3883 ext. 231

world wide web
www.dpibooks.com